1981

Let Me Do It!

ANNE ROGOVIN

With an Introduction by Dr. Benjamin Spock

A John Day Book

THOMAS Y. CROWELL, PUBLISHERS

NEW YORK

Established 1834

This book surely would never have been possible without my wonderful husband, Milton. I lovingly dedicate this book to him

our children
>> Ellen (and Jack)
>> Paula (and Peter)
>> Mark (and Helen)

our grandchildren
>> Malaika
>> David
>> Steven
>> Aliya

and all the children on this planet
for a world of peace and freedom.

Photographs by Anne and Milton Rogovin

FIRST EDITION

Designed by Lydia Link

Library of Congress Cataloging in Publication Data

Rogovin, Anne.
  Let me do it !
  SUMMARY: Suggestions for games, projects, and activities using materials easily available around the house or in nature. Includes ideas for fingerplays, puppet shows, stoveless cooking, gardening, handicraft projects, and more.
  1. Creative activities and seat work. 2. Amusements. 3. Indoor games. [1. Amusements. I. Title.
GV1203.R583   649'.51   78-3316
ISBN 0-381-98300-5
ISBN 0-381-98301-3 pbk.

80 81 82 83 84 10 9 8 7 6 5 4 3 2 1

CONTENTS

INTRODUCTION

A Bit of Advice to Parents from Ben Spock

I am—and always was—an unimaginative parent and grandparent myself. When my children asked me to tell a story, my mind went blank. And if I forced myself to begin with: "Once upon a time there were two little boys," I could only think of ultrarealistic actions like "and they went to school in the morning," which didn't make a very interesting tale. For a project for my child, I could buy a solid model airplane kit, but that's not anything you can procure on the spur of the moment—or without money.

When I and my four sisters and one brother were children, the most popular books in the house were a many-volumed set for children that was partly encyclopedia, partly stories, and partly do-it-yourself directions for such projects as making a miniature farm, or building a real electric bell out of a tin can and a worn-out electromagnet that your neighborhood electrician will sell you "for a few cents." I read all these directions avidly. I made the simpler things that needed only materials already available in our house. But I rarely had the few cents to get the necessary extras, and I rather doubted that the electrician would have the worn-out electromagnet or would welcome my trade.

Anne Rogovin's book *Let Me Do It !* will be a great success with your children. It will be just as great a success with you. It's a fat book all full of ingenious things that your *young* child can do, or can make out of things that are in *any* home, no matter how modest: animals to keep, not only puppies from the pound but insects, too; what to make with empty plastic bottles; how to make puppets and put on a show; tasty recipes a child can make without a stove; how to grow simple plants (which fascinates all children); how to make a musical instrument; what to do with spools, tires, yarn, stones, and rope; and about water, sand, and mud pies.

With this book your child will never run out of projects, and you'll always have an answer when your child says, "There's nothing to *do !*" This is indeed a wonderful and necessary book, and the most significant work ever written on the subject.

Benjamin Spock, M.D.

There was a child went forth every day;
And the first object he looked upon and received with wonder,
      pity, love, or dread,
that object he became.

—WALT WHITMAN,
      "There Was a Child Went Forth"

A LETTER TO PARENTS

Perhaps there are exceptions, but I have never heard of parents who did not want the best for their child—that it grow up to be healthy physically and mentally and a useful self-sufficient member of society. All of us want this for our children, but it isn't always easy the way things are—and sometimes we can use a little help. I hope this book will help in some small way.

But please do not look upon me as an authority. I am, and have been, a classroom teacher for many years and am a parent of three grown children, each of whom is living and teaching in the inner cities of New York, Philadelphia, and Chicago. Each loves and knows a great deal about trees, flowers, birds, and such things, but chooses to be in the cities, where their help is needed so badly. And, of course, I am very proud of this.

My husband is an optometrist, but he spends most of his extra time photographing and documenting the lives of the poor. He photographs them with compassion and the dignity we both feel they deserve.

May I make a few other comments? You, of course, would like to know what age range this book is for. It is rather hard to say, because all children are different. But I would say . . . the beginning age is just about at the time when a tiny child is snuggled in its parent's arms, or perhaps when it hears its first soft lullaby. All the way to the age when that child stops liking to play with water or wanting a story before bedtime.

- It may be for a child with no serious problems ("normal"?)
- For a child who is blind
- Or a child with deep emotional problems ("learning disabilities"?)
- Or the very poor ("the disadvantaged"?)
- Or one who learns very slowly ("retarded"?)
  Each growing at his or her own rate of speed and *not being pressed by anyone, however well meaning.*

It is my very strong belief that the principles of learning are generally the same for most of these children (whatever they may be considered) and that most of them learn best by doing and working at those things that are relevant and important to them.

You may notice that the activities and materials used throughout the book are very simple, easily available in our homes or nearby—and are noncompetitive. This is good, I believe, for they help bring exciting challenges and more lasting satisfactions to the child—and society in general.

You may see, too, that things from nature are commonly suggested; for it seems to me that there ought to be a sympathy with common things, a kind of harmony with our environment, an understanding that nature (despite the crowded cities, the pollution, etc.) is all around us, sending out messages to us begging us to pay attention:

- light
- the stars
- a fresh breeze
- a yellow dandelion
- a worm brought out by the rain
- seeds
- leaves
- pigeons on a fire escape
- squirrels scampering up a tree
- clouds
- rain

Dear Parents, take whatever you will from this book. Thumb through it from time to time. See if there is anything you think might be helpful. Have fun and enjoy every minute with your child, for childhood goes by very quickly.

Yours

Anne Rogovin

Anne Rogovin

My deepest appreciation to Dr. Clifford N. Crooks (District Superintendent of the Board of Cooperative Educational Services, Number 1) for granting me a Sabbatical Leave of Absence from my teaching in order to complete my book.

ANIMALS

Given a choice of anything in the world they would like to have most of all—more than dolls, more than a bicycle or an electric train—my guess is that the majority of children would like to have a live animal pet.

Luckily for children, ducks are terrible runners but can waddle about (oh, so delightfully awkward), making good company for children to talk to.

A rabbit

is for

loving

And feeding

And to draw

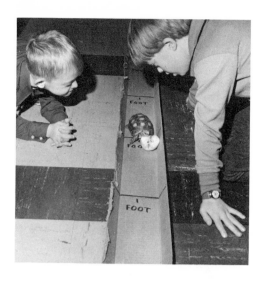

As long as children aren't *made* to (do you remember the book reports you *had* to make after you read a book?), they can be encouraged to make their own interesting observations.

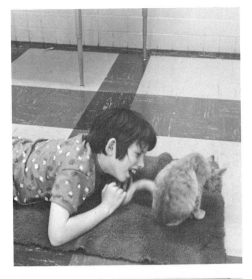

The local SPCA or dog pound usually has unwanted or stray animals you might get as pets.

If you can't own a pet, you can have a temporary pet as we have, when our school aide brings hers to school. You might have a friend going away on vacation whose pet you can "borrow."

When you have a male guinea pig and a female guinea pig (unfortunately Sally got camera-shy and is behind the blocks), you can be sure that you will have some dynamic lessons in "life."

The poor snake has more myths and misconceptions about it than just about any living thing.

No, they aren't all poisonous.

No, snakes aren't slimy. Their scales are perfectly dry.

No, when a snake thrusts out its tongue, it isn't trying to bite you, it's only trying to find out what's going on.

A "found" sparrow—and a call to the Museum of Science tells us "what to do."

The big, beautiful monarch butterfly is just a visitor. *(You wouldn't want to be locked up in a cage, would you? The butterfly wants to be free. It has a lot of work to do.)*

5

BAGS

When Michelle picks a sneaker out of one bag and concentrates hard to feel for a matching sneaker in the other bag, she is training her sense of touch.

Seeing, hearing, tasting, smelling, touching. What marvelous instruments nature has given us !

When children live with these senses sharpened every minute of the day, of the year

wherever they may be

- at school
- at home
- in the neighborhood
- in the country

whatever the weather

- rain
- hail
- sunshine
- or snow

what a tremendous collection of information and sensations can be piled up to make a child's life alive and rich !

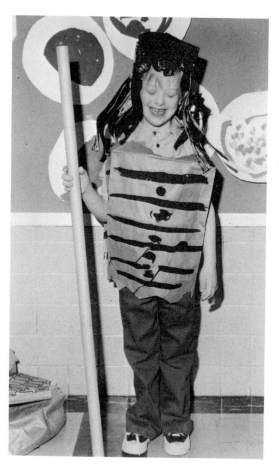

Don't you agree that Michael
makes a magnificent leader
for the parade?

Michael could have used another
bag to make a mask for his face,
but he didn't want one.

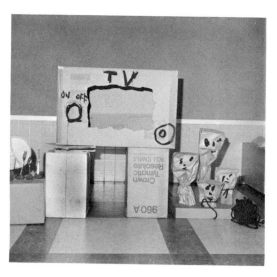

This attractive set of puppets is
a child's "family," and they are
about to go to the restaurant
for a lesson on "pleases" and
"thank yous."

"Time to put your things away" can be more pleasant for a child when large paper shopping bags are labeled and easily accessible.

Before you buy a game, why not see if you could make it, or something like it. Better yet, could your child make it "all by myself"?

What else can you use for tossing besides buttons?

- stones?
- chestnuts?
- bottle tops?
- peanuts?

8

BIRDS

Do you know that the beautiful wild outdoor birds—like robins, sparrows, chickadees, and dozens of others—can be a child's special pets? Very special indeed, because the birds can roam about happy and completely free, with no cages to bar them.

Let your child try to lure these fast-moving creatures to come closer, stop awhile, and have a bite to eat. It's not so hard to do if you use bird feeders (one, two, three, or more lunch counters full of food they love, like birdseed, bread crumbs, suet, raisins, and peanut butter). Be sure to include water, because birds get thirsty, as all of us do.

And another thing to remember, put the bird feeders out of the way of cats, who will eat up the food—and maybe the birds too !

How to Attract Birds

JUST-A-DISH FEEDER

Put food on a dish and set it in a spot where cats and other animals can't get at it.

GOURD FEEDER

Cut a hole in the gourd. Put table scraps into hole and suspend from branch.

BERRY-BASKET FEEDER

Put cord through holes of berry basket. Add suet and suspend.

TIN-CAN FEEDER

Remove top and bottom of tin can. Put cord through and suspend.

ALUMINUM-FOIL PIE-PLATE FEEDER

Poke three holes close to the rim of a pie plate. Put cord through holes and suspend.

PLASTIC-BOTTLE BIRD FEEDER

Cut out half of side of plastic bottle. Leave the bottom to set food on. Suspend.

WALNUT SHELL

Suspend walnut shell with peanut butter.

GRAPEFRUIT (OR ORANGE) FEEDER

Poke two or three holes through grapefruit (or orange). Put cord through holes and suspend.

DOUGHNUT

Hang doughnut from string.

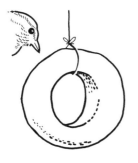

POPCORN AND CRANBERRIES

Lace popcorn and cranberries onto string. Suspend.

CORN FEEDER

Attach corn onto string and suspend from branch.

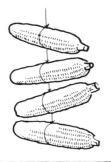

SUNFLOWER-PLANT FEEDER

Grow sunflowers and watch birds come for their seeds at the end of the summer.

BIRDS

BOTTLES

BIRD-NEST SUPPLIES

Mount supplies for bird nest (string, yarn) in slits of paper tube.

ONION BAGS

Stuff onion bag or cheesecloth with suet and suspend from branch.

PAINT WITH PEANUT BUTTER

Paint peanut butter on tree with knife or stick.

SUET

Tie suet on tree.

PINE-CONE FEEDER

Stuff pine cone with peanut butter and suspend from branch.

LID FOR WATER

Place lid upside down with water.

BOTTLES

It really isn't of great importance that a child know what sound *this* seed or *that* seed makes when it's jiggled in the jar. What *is* important is for the child to get in the habit of listening carefully.

Listen to

- rain on the windowpane
- car horns
- a factory whistle
- the snap of a twig
- footsteps on the sidewalk
  (Are they all the same?)
- the crunch of an apple
- the robin *(Can you imitate her song?)*
- the grass *(Does it whisper?)*

Can you close your eyes and imagine the sound of

- a hammer
- sweeping
- water from the faucet
- sawing wood
- the doorbell
- the eggbeater
- cutting with scissors
- the pencil sharpener

How many of these sounds can you make?

- cry
- sigh
- cough
- hum
- swallow
- pant
- sneeze
- choke
- whisper
- sing
- blow
- sniff

Can you giggle? Can you snore?

13

An exciting toss game made of pop bottles and canning-ring rubbers gives no hint that you are encouraging your child to enjoy things that have to do with numbers.

When Maureen holds "the woods" she made all by herself

the fir twigs, the damp earth and the berries *she* gathered
the jar *she* got from a neighbor
the cover *she* put on to "watch the droplets collect under the glass and see how they drop back again to water the earth"

she will remember this for a long time.

14

When you go "up the hill," you can tell *by yourself* when the bottle isn't the right size—and you can make the correction *by yourself.*

It looks as though Maureen is just sorting nails, doesn't it? No, Maureen is doing much more. She is making comparisons, forming judgments, reasoning, and making decisions. (I wish you could have seen the look of triumph when her job was completed !)

These bottles (and cans) painted with *your own colors* and *your own designs* give you another chance to feel, "I'm satisfied with what I did !"

Can you write your name with bottle tops? Your telephone number?

Can you draw a pretty picture with bottle tops?

15

BOXES

It doesn't take long to transform a large carton from the supermarket into a car, train, plane, or boat. (And no reservations needed !)

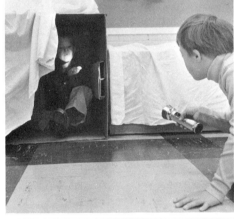

An extra-large carton from a big appliance makes an inviting hideaway house.

Assorted sizes make magnificent towers for "building up" and "knocking down" (also for "getting into").

16

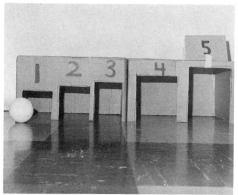

A child usually won't need coaxing to do number work with such an enticing bowling alley as this.

You don't have a ball handy? Then, roll up a sock and use that.

Not many children would refuse to match numbers with these dice made from half-pint milk cartons. Milk cartons also can make:

- a set of blocks (especially good if you have other sizes like quarts, half gallons, and gallons)
- containers for growing seeds

When Michael puts a slit on the cover of the large-size oatmeal box, it will become a bank, "so I can save my money for a bicycle."

Other round boxes, like those from cheese and ice-cream, make excellent treasure boxes for stones and marbles.

The oatmeal and mothball boxes are "the City Hall," and the toilet tissue rolls are a "little house."

17

A supply of shoe boxes helps keep things in order. Children may need a certain amount of order (perhaps more than we adults realize). Order gives children something they can "count on" and can be psychologically satisfying.

Fruit boxes, bottle tops, buttons, spools, scissors (things within a child's environment) make early contacts with numbers pleasant.

BRICKS

You can make a house with bricks, "just like big people."
Bricks are especially good because

- A child has practice "being careful so they don't fall on you and hurt you."

- They are heavy and require effort to pick up.

- They can be outdoors all the time and you don't have to worry about anything spoiling them.

Bricks are wonderful to paint on because the texture is so rough.

- If your door won't stay open, you can have your child paint a brick and use it as a doorstop.
- If you need book ends, paint two bricks.
- If you need a bookcase or shelves for toys, don't forget that you can use bricks to hold up the horizontal boards.

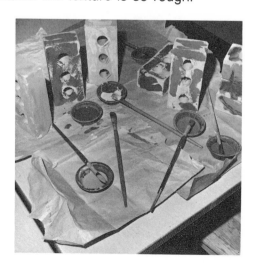

BUTTONS

Do you have hundreds of buttons in your button box waiting to be used "someday"? Your child will be delighted to use them *now,* for sorting into different colors and sizes.

Beads are good to use too if you have big ones.

Did you ever "draw" a picture with buttons?

Did you ever have a button necklace and/or a matching bracelet?

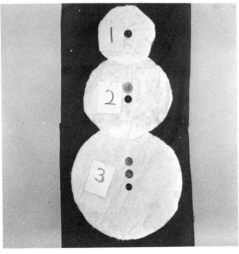

Buttons can be used to make into a Hit-the-Snowman game, with a child anxious to "add up" scores.

Another good game is the Button Toss game, where you stand away from a shoe box (or you can use a hat if you want to) and see how many buttons you can throw into it.

CANS

Although the clatter may be a little hard on parents, empty cans (gathered at home or from restaurants) can make a child's paradise. May I suggest that if the noise gets too intolerable, an old blanket will help to muffle the sound.

Usually canned goods stored in the pantry come in different sizes. This is good. Then you can use them for stacking (setting on top of one another) and for nesting (fitting into one another, when they are empty).

Or the canned goods can be used for sorting different colors, examining pictures, looking at the words, etc.

This great city (with its houses and tall buildings) was made with assorted cans and other round boxes.

These coffee cans with clothespins snapped on top are for "number study." They can be used for other things like

Book ends: Put a plant in each of two empty cans and fill extra space with small stones.

Totem pole: Put two, three, or more cans on top of each other with masking tape. Put faces on if you want to.

You can do everything with 33mm film cans that you can do with bigger cans, *but can you put bigger cans on your fingers like this?*

Can you make a family of finger puppets?

CARDBOARD

A good way to get *boys* and girls started in sewing is to make a gigantic sewing card of cardboard and use thick yarn for "thread."

CANS

CARDBOARD

A large piece of cardboard with slits cut into it for weaving paper, cloth, or ribbon "in and out" makes a hanging that would enliven any wall.

The best thing about making your own puzzles (besides, of course, that they don't cost anything) is that they can be custom-made. Even a one-year-old might be able to work a two-piece puzzle of a pie or a ball. As the child gets older, the puzzle can get harder and harder with five, ten, or more pieces !

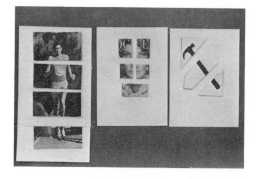

All you need to do is to select a picture from a newspaper, magazine, or old book, cut it out, mount it on a piece of cardboard, and then cut the board into as many pieces as you wish. Use a bag or an envelope so the pieces don't get lost or mixed up with another puzzle.

Can you make a puzzle of your child's name? If it's TOM, the puzzle can be made from three parts: T, O, and M. Can you make a puzzle from your address?

CLAY

"It's such a great feeling to do things with my hands,
And it doesn't bother me one bit that they get messy. . . .
I even like the mess !
It's such a great feeling to do things with my hands,
Because what I make is all mine . . . .
It makes me feel so good inside. . . .
I don't get tired, . . .
And I want to go
On . . .
And on . . .
And on . . .
And on . . .
And never stop."

24

Clay is very good for making things. You can do anything you want with it. You can

- push it
- poke it
- pat it
- roll it

- punch it
- twist it
- squeeze it
- smooth it

The best thing about clay is that you can start out with just a big glob of it—and you will always turn out with something different from anyone else's !

You might be able to find some natural clay in the neighborhood where you live—perhaps at a construction site. If you do, ask one of the workers if you can have a little for your child to play with. If he says OK (which he probably will), put a little in a plastic bag so it will stay soft and moist, ready for "instant" use.

Also, if you have a garden, you might want to consider taking an out-of-the-way corner, digging out a hole, filling it with water—and letting your child have a glorious mudhole for pies and other de-li-cious things !

Don't mind the mess, because mud is very easy to wash off.

CLOTHING

Almost anything you might want to discard (old clothing, worn-out sheets and pillowcases, tablecloths, curtains, etc.) can transform a child into a ballerina, a bride, a clown, "mommy," "daddy," or a truck driver.

Just a scarf will make a child "be somebody else." It doesn't take much to give a child's imagination a chance to work.

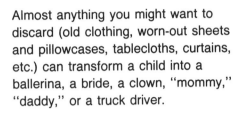

Dumped into the pretend box (a handy bushel basket), the "costumes" are always ready for impromptu play and are easy to put away when through.

Other baskets can be used for storing dolls and blocks, making cleanup time a quick, palatable experience.

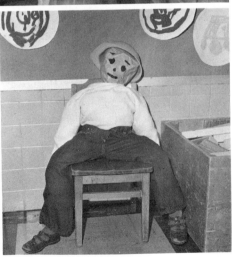

A life-size doll (made from stuffed clothing and a paper bag for a head) can be a child's "best friend" on a rainy day.

26

When Michelle sorts the wash, she is learning about the personal joys that could come from work—and the social good for the family. If Michelle doesn't learn this *now*—it may be too late when she is older.

"Hanging out the wash" can give dramatic attention to seeing. See the difference in

- shapes
- colors
- material

What else can you learn?

A child may practice shoe-tying, buckling, or zipping more enthusiastically on these mannequins (discarded by a neighboring dress shop) than if told, "Now, boys and girls —it's time to work on tying shoes."

(How children love excitement and drama !)

27

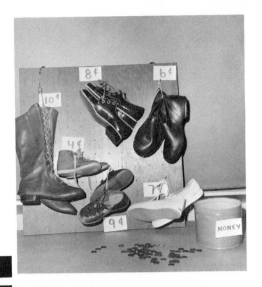

Boots, shoes, rubbers, and sneakers can be used to "play store" for fun and incidentally motivate the need for learning basic math, etc.

CLOTHING

DANCE

These same items can be matched and used as a lotto game,

Or they can be used to develop the concept of pairs.

If you have socks or mittens handy, use these too.

DANCE

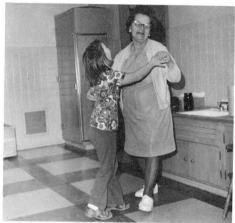

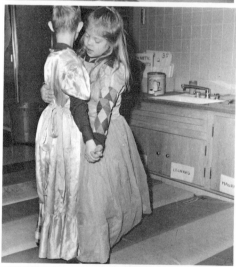

DANCE EDUCATION BEGINS

- when you dance with Mom (or Dad) before breakfast or before going to bed at night

CLOTHING

DANCE

- when you put on a long dress and dance with your sister or brother or a playmate

- when you've had enough of what you had to do and decide to
    kick
        whirl and twirl
            fly
                leap
    Be a butterfly
        a snowflake
        a gentle rain
        a top

Can you reach up and get an apple?

Can you "dance a flower opening up and reaching for the sun"?

Can you "dance your name"?

When we dance, we "talk with our bodies." What would you like to "talk about"?

- a kite
- a tree in the wind
- a jack-in-the-box
- a child learning to walk
- picking berries
- climbing a steep cliff
- building a house with bricks
- your father's work
- your mother's work
- Jack-Be-Nimble
- Little Miss Muffet
- a rolling ball
- a gentle wind
- a hurricane
- touching the sky
- being very small
- a "Raggedy Ann" doll
- a robot
- jelly
- a feather
- being very tired
- being very happy
- being very strong
- Humpty Dumpty
- playing the piano
- typewriting
- a rubber band
- kittens sleeping by the fireplace
- floating on a cloud
- wilting flower
- a candle burning down

- an ice-cream cone
- a traffic guard
- a bicycle
- stroking a cat
- a windmill
- a hoop
- a butterfly
- an airplane
- rowing a boat
- a mechanical doll
- an octopus
- chopping wood
- turning into a statue
- an accordion
- a galloping pony
- running between raindrops
- picking apples
- moving like a snake
- walking on soft, cool grass
- walking on red-hot pavement
- springing like a grasshopper
- a kangaroo
- climbing a tree
- the orchestra leader
- a choppy sea
- being lost
- Cinderella at the ball
- a scarecrow
- a top
- a circle

DANCE

FINGER PLAYS

FINGER PLAYS

The lilt and the simple motions of finger plays make them very special for a child. You can have a conversation with each other long before the child even knows words.

But please, *at no time* force a child to take part.

If you have a good time doing a finger play, watch your child. It almost becomes contagious—and, before you know it, your child will automatically have a good time too.

DANCE

FINGER PLAY

There are other advantages to doing finger plays. For example, they help to teach meanings of abstract concepts like "up and down," number concepts, parts of the body, etc.

They help to develop a sense of rhythm, the imagination—but mostly **finger plays are for fun and talking together.**

LET'S MAKE BALLS

A little ball

FINGER PLAYS

A bigger ball

A great big ball I see

Now let's count the balls

One
Two
Three !

32

EVERYBODY DO THIS

Everybody do this
     do this
     do this
Everybody do this
     do this
     do this
Just like me (point to self)

(Same as above with
  fingers-hopping action)

(Same as above with
  arms-flying action)

Etc.

TEN LITTLE FINGERS

I have ten little fingers,   And they all belong to me.

FINGER PLAYS

I can make them do things.
Would you like to see?

I can open them wide.
I can shut them up tight.

I can put them together
Or make them all hide.
I can make them go high,
I can make them go low.
I can hold them quietly
Or fold them just so.

34

THE BEEHIVE

	Directions
Here's a little beehive.	Make a fist.
Where are the bees?	Examine the beehive.
Hidden away	
Where nobody sees.	
Here they come creeping	
Out of the hive.	
1-2-3-4-5	Bring out one finger at a time.
Bzzzzzzzzzzzzzzzzzzz	Fingers fly away.

MY TURTLE

	Directions
This is my turtle.	Make a fist. Extend thumb.
He lives in a shell.	Hide thumb in fist.
He likes his home	
Very well.	
He pokes his head out	
When he wants to eat.	Extend thumb.
And pulls back in	
When he wants to sleep.	Hide thumb in fist.

TWO LITTLE BLACKBIRDS

	Directions
Two little blackbirds	Put both hands behind back.
Sitting on a wall,	
One named Peter,	Bring right hand forward with thumb up.
The other named Paul.	Bring left hand forward with thumb up.
Fly away, Peter.	Put right hand behind back.
Fly away, Paul.	Put left hand behind back.
Come back, Peter.	Bring right hand forward with thumb up.
Come back, Paul.	Bring left hand forward with thumb up.

THE BUS

Directions

The wheels on the bus go round and round
round and round
round and round
The wheels on the bus go round and round
All day long.

Raise hands and make them roll one after the other in a big circle.

More verses include:

The people on the bus go up and down, etc.

Stand up and down.

The money on the bus goes clink, clank, clink, etc.

Drop money in container.

The driver on the bus says, "Move on back," etc.

Motion to back of bus with hand.

The children on the bus say, "Yack, yack, yack," etc.

Children cry.

The mothers on the bus say, "Sh, sh, sh," etc.

Put finger to lips and make "sh" sound.

The wipers on the bus go, "Swish, swish, swish," etc.

Make round motion with hands.

The horn on the bus says, "Honk, honk, honk," etc.

Make pressing motion with thumb.

The wheels on the bus go "round and round," etc.

Raise hands and make them roll together in a big circle.

RAIN

Directions

Rain is coming down.
Rain is coming down.
Down. Down.
Down. Down.
Rain is coming down.

Raise hands high in the air with fingers pointing downward. Lower hands gradually until they touch the ground.

More verses include:

snow
hail
leaves

THE APPLE TREE

Directions

Way up high in the apple tree   Make a circle with hands above head.
Two little apples smiled at me.
I shook that tree as hard as I could.   Shake hands vigorously.
Down came the apples.   Drop hands.
Mmmm—they were good !   Rub stomach.

TWO LITTLE HOUSES

Directions

Two little houses closed up tight.   Hold up two fists.
Open the windows   Spread open the fingers.
And let in the light.

TEN LITTLE CHILDREN

Directions

One little, two little, three little children;   Extend a finger with each number.
Four little, five little, six little children;
Seven little, eight little, nine little children;
Ten little children all.

THIS IS MY RIGHT HAND

Directions

This is my right hand.   Fit action to words.
I'll raise it up high.
This is my left hand.
I'll touch the sky.

CHICKADEES

Directions

Five little chickadees sitting on the floor.
One flew away and then there were four.
Four little chickadees sitting on a tree.
One flew away and then there were three.
Three little chickadees looking at you.
One flew away and then there were two.
Two little chickadees sitting in the sun.
One flew away and then there was one.
One little chickadee sitting all alone.
It flew away and then there were none.

Hold up hand with fingers extended.
Fold down each finger as the bird flies
away.

FINGER PLAYS

FOOD

OPEN, SHUT THEM

Directions

Open, shut them; open, shut them.
Give a little clap.
Open, shut them; open, shut them.
Put them on your lap.

Using hands and fingers, fit action to
words.

FOOD

Are you ever in doubt about *what to do* for a child and *what not to do?* It isn't easy to decide, because we as adults can do things faster, neater —and it's oh, so hard to be patient sometimes !

Yet, it is terribly important for a child to have work to do. In a real sense, a child who isn't given work can be considered a deprived child and is likely to show the results of this sooner or later.

There is one very good motto to keep in mind. This is it: "Try not to do for a child what the child can do for himself or herself." Try this advice as consistently as possible—you may find it remarkably useful !

How many of these things is your child trained to do *consistently* and *willingly?*

- scrub carrots
- scrub beets
- husk corn
- shell peas
- tear lettuce
- snap beans
- wash fruit
- set table
- clear dishes from table
- rinse, wash, dry dishes and put them away
- polish silverware
- sort silverware
- take out garbage
- sweep floor

- vacuum rug
- dust furniture
- make bed
- polish shoes
- sort and match socks
- empty and clean drawers
- rake leaves
- sweep sidewalk and driveway
- shovel snow
- put toys away
- mail letters
- water plants
- help hang wash
- help mow lawn
- run simple errands

Is there something your child can do for a neighbor?

Children are like little birds—they always seem to be hungry.

Why not have them learn to prepare simple dishes themselves —but only those dishes that don't need *stoves, blenders, can openers,* and other such things that could be dangerous. They can use these when they are older and more responsible.

Here are some very, very easy recipes that are healthful (and tasty too !) and can be made entirely by the child.

Go through them—step by step—and someday you might find your child volunteering to make his or her own lunch (or part of it).

CHOCOLATE MILKSHAKE

What You Need

  1 cup milk
  1 tablespoon chocolate syrup
  1 jar with lid

What to Do

  1. Put milk and syrup in jar.
  2. Put lid on jar.
  3. Shake well.
  4. Serve.

BANANA SHAKE

What You Need

  1 banana
  1 cup milk
  1 jar with lid

What to Do

  1. Mash banana with fork.
  2. Put banana in jar.
  3. Add milk.
  4. Put lid on jar.
  5. Shake well.
  6. Serve.

It's fun to stuff celery and lick the fingers when you're done.

STUFFED CELERY

What You Need

celery stalk
cream cheese

What to Do

1. Stuff hollow of celery with cream cheese, using dull knife.
2. Serve.

CARROT AND RAISIN SALAD

What You Need

1 carrot
a few raisins
1 lettuce leaf
mayonnaise

What to Do

1. Cut carrot into bite-size pieces.
2. Add raisins.
3. Mix with mayonnaise.
4. Put on lettuce leaf.
5. Serve.

CREAM CHEESE AND LETTUCE ROLL

What You Need

cream cheese
lettuce leaf

What to Do

1. Spread cream cheese on lettuce leaf with dull knife.
2. Roll up lettuce leaf.
3. Serve.

It takes young Christine a very long time to make up the cottage cheese salad. *"I want to make it just right."*

COTTAGE CHEESE SALAD

What You Need

1 cup cottage cheese
1 lettuce leaf

What to Do

1. Put cottage cheese on lettuce.
2. Serve.

Variation: Add bite-size pieces of vegetables or fruit.
Also, nuts.

COTTAGE CHEESE

Instead of throwing out milk that has soured, why not have your child make cottage cheese from it? It's very easy. Here's all you do:

What You Need

soured milk
cheesecloth
cold water
spoon

What to Do

1. Keep the soured milk in a warm place (not hot) until you see that the hard part (curd) is separated from the soft part (whey).
2. Pour it through the cheesecloth.
3. Press the hard part with a spoon to squeeze out the liquid.
4. Pour cold water through.

What's left is cottage cheese !

FRUIT SALAD

What You Need

1 lettuce leaf
fresh fruit (apples, peaches, pears, etc.)

What to Do

1. Cut fruit into bite-size pieces.
2. Place fruit on lettuce leaf.
3. Serve.

42

Maureen has been shown *(step by step)* over and over again the correct way to make a sandwich. Now she can boast, *"I can do it all by myself !"*

AMERICAN CHEESE SANDWICH

What You Need

2 slices bread (preferably
  whole-wheat)
1 or 2 slices American cheese
mustard or mayonnaise

What to Do

1. Put cheese on one slice of bread.
2. Spread mustard or mayonnaise on other slice.
3. Close with second slice.
4. Serve.

Variation: Use Swiss cheese.

PEANUT BUTTER SANDWICH

What You Need

peanut butter
2 slices bread (preferably
  whole-wheat)

What to Do

1. Spread peanut butter on one slice of bread.
2. Close sandwich with second slice.
3. Serve.

Variation: Follow above directions and add jelly for a peanut butter and jelly sandwich.

43

Do you want a treat for the whole family that was made by your child—a delicious, healthful treat? Then make your very own butter. It's so easy and such fun !

FOOD

BUTTER

What You Need

> pint of heavy cream
> jar with lid
> a little salt

What to Do

1. Put the cream in the jar. Cover with lid. Let it stand until it reaches room temperature.
2. Shake jar until butter forms.
3. Pour out remaining liquid.
4. Rinse butter in cold water.
5. Add a little salt, if you wish.

Then get it on some nice fresh bread as fast as you can !

WHEAT-GERM BANANA SNACK

What You Need

> 1 banana
> wheat germ

What to Do

1. Cut banana into circles or strips.
2. Dip pieces into wheat germ.
3. Serve.

CREAM-CHEESE-BALL SNACK

What You Need

> 1 package cream cheese

What to Do

1. Roll cream cheese into balls.
2. Serve.

Variations: Roll balls in cut-up walnuts.
Roll balls in sesame seeds.

FRUITED HONEY SNACKS

What You Need

> honey
> jar with tight lid
> fruit:
> > whole (grapes, strawberries)
> > sliced (apples, pears, peaches, etc.)

What to Do

1. Place fruit in jar.
2. Cover fruit with honey.
3. Store in refrigerator.
4. Serve.

Have you ever come across a child who did not love raisins? I *never* have ! Let your child make a supply of raisins to wrap up in individual plastic packages or little boxes—ready to eat (instead of candy).

RAISINS

What You Need

grapes

What to Do

1. Put grapes on a sunny window sill.
2. Turn them over once in a while.
3. Wait a few days and the raisins will be ready to be devoured.

RAISIN AND SUNFLOWER-SEED SNACK

What You Need

a handful of raisins
a handful of sunflower seeds

What to Do

1. Mix raisins and sunflower seeds.
2. Serve.

Variation: Follow same directions and use walnuts instead of sunflower seeds.

FOOD

CHOCOLATE PUDDING

What You Need

1 package instant chocolate pudding
2 cups milk
jar with lid

What to Do

1. Put milk and pudding in jar.
2. Put lid on jar.
3. Shake until pudding thickens.
4. Serve.

INSTANT PUDDING WHIP

What You Need

1 package instant pudding
2 cups warm water

What to Do

1. Empty pudding into bowl.
2. Add 2 cups warm water. Stir.
3. Set in refrigerator for several hours.
4. Serve.

FRUIT JUICE POPSICLES

What You Need

fruit juice (orange, grapefruit, or grape)
paper cups
sticks

What to Do

1. Pour juice into cups.
2. Put in freezer.
3. Add sticks when juice starts to harden.
4. Serve when frozen.

FRUITED ICE CUBES

What You Need

fruit juice (orange, grapefruit, or grape)
ice-cube tray

What to Do

1. Fill ice-cube tray with fruit juice.
2. Put tray in freezer.
3. After fruit is frozen, remove a cube and place in a glass.
4. Add water.
5. Serve.

LEMONADE

What You Need

1 lemon
2 tablespoons sugar or honey
1 glass water

What to Do

1. Squeeze lemon to get 2 tablespoons of juice.
2. Pour juice into glass.
3. Add sugar or honey and water.
4. Stir and serve.

Playing store with *real merchandise* and *real money* is chock-full of dynamic learning experiences for a child. It gives practice in

- "Making change"
- "Waiting your turn"
- The "thank yous" and "pleases"

When Jimmy has a firsthand, on-the-spot taste of a lemon, he is sharpening his sense of taste, (one more way to find out about the things in the world about him).

Here are some other things for tasting:

- raw peas
- grass
- olives
- a dill pickle
- tomatoes, warm from the sun
- clover blossoms
- dandelion greens
- snow
- an icicle

Did you ever taste rain caught on your tongue?

As simple as this little lemonade stand appears, it involves a lot of:

- choosing
- ordering
- paying for
- getting change
- being polite
- cooperating
- finding out a little more about people

"Bananas are yellow. A lemon is yellow. Grapefruit is yellow."

You can take a "yellow walk" around the house to find other things that are yellow. You can also go around the block for a "yellow walk."

We learn *one thing* very, very well, enjoying the little successes that come from successful repetitions. Once we have these "good feelings" of accomplishment, we happily go on to learn something else.

"Shall we see what fruits are red? Strawberries? Grapes?"

FOOD

FURNITURE

Floors are just as good a place for a child to learn on as a table or a desk.

Jimmy and John are rolling grapefruit with a spoon. No, they aren't trying to see "who gets there first." Each is trying to "get there"— period ! We just want lots of little personal successes. So often, competition means someone has failed.

FURNITURE

For matters of utmost privacy, a table with an old curtain thrown over it could hardly be better.

The legs of an upside-down chair are perfect for an impromptu ring-toss game.

49

INSECTS

It would be hard to find a hobby that is much easier than collecting insects. Did you know that there are over 900,000 kinds that are *known*—and more are being found all the time? Yes !

You can find insects just about everywhere:

- in every room in every house
- in the yard (There may be as many as 500 different ones there *right now.*)
- in every room in every school
- in the garage (Look in your car too.)
- in the air
- underneath every stone
- in every drop of water

In fact, there's hardly a place where they aren't. It requires very little effort to find a few to become our friends.

Oh yes—one bit of very important advice. When your child becomes disinterested in the insect pet, please don't kill it. Let it go outside.

ANT HOUSE

What You Need

jar
soil
food (crumbs, sweet water)
black paper or cardboard
a piece of old wood or a twig
ants

What to Do

1. Put soil in jar.
2. Add ants, wood, and food.
3. Put paper alongside of jar.
4. Put lid on jar.

*When you want to watch the ants work,
take off the black paper.*

BUTTERFLY HOUSE

What You Need

gallon jug
food (leaves, mashed fruit, sweetened
    water)
butterfly

What to Do

1. Add butterfly and food to jug.
2. Put holes in lid for air.

*If you can find a cocoon and watch the
butterfly emerge, that is a thrilling thing to see !*

CATERPILLAR HOUSE

What You Need

plastic bag with air holes
leaves on which the caterpillar was
    found
caterpillar

What to Do

Wrap and tie plastic bag around leaves
and caterpillar. Watch the caterpillar weave
its cocoon.

COCKROACH CAGE

What You Need

    ice-cream or cottage-cheese carton
    sticky plastic wrap
    bread crumbs
    cockroach

What to Do

1. Cut out window in carton.
2. Cover window with sticky plastic wrap.
3. Add food and cockroach to carton.
4. Put lid on.

The cockroach may be a nuisance in the kitchen but it really is a very interesting creature to watch. See how it cleans its legs.

What You Need

    jar
    flowerpot
    soil
    lettuce leaves, bread, cereal
    cricket

What to Do

1. Fill pot with soil.
2. Place jar over pot.
3. Add leaves, cricket, etc.

CRICKET CAGE

Listen ! See how it scrapes one wing across the edge of the other. Chiiirrruup ! Chiiirrruuup !

DADDY LONGLEGS HOUSE

What You Need

    carton
    screening or cheesecloth
    food (sweetened water)
    daddy longlegs

What to Do

1. Cut out side of carton.
2. Cover with screening or cheesecloth
3. Add sweetened water and daddy longlegs.

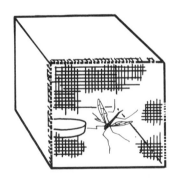

Watch "daddy" wash his legs.

FIREFLY HOUSE

What You Need

jar
screening or cheesecloth
food (leaves and drops of water for a
  drink)
firefly

What to Do

1. Put firefly and food into jar.
2. Cover top with screening or
   cheesecloth.

*At night place jar on table (near your bed)
and watch the firefly's little lights blink on
and off—on and off—on and off.*

FLY HOUSE

What You Need

drinking glass
food (crumbs, drops of water for a drink)
fly

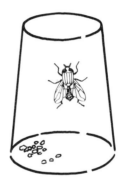

What to Do

1. Turn glass upside down.
2. Enclose food and fly.

See how wonderfully the fly is made.

GRASSHOPPER HOUSE

What You Need

potted plant
screening or cheesecloth
food (bread crumbs, bits of fruit and
  drops of water for a drink)
grasshopper

What to Do

1. Sew or staple screening or
   cheesecloth around plant.
2. Add food and grasshopper.

*Watch grasshopper hop about from leaf to
leaf.*

LADYBUG HOUSE

What You Need

goldfish bowl
screening or cheesecloth
food (dried-up yellow leaves, which
usually have aphids on) and some
drops of water for a drink
ladybug

What to Do

1. Put ladybug and food in bowl.
2. Cover with screening or cheesecloth.

Turn ladybug over on her back and see how she "plays dead."

Watch—and then see how she suddenly turns and scurries away !

MILLIPEDE HOUSE

What You Need

water pitcher
food (leaves, drops of water for a
drink)
screening or cheesecloth
millipede

What to Do

1. Put leaves, food, and millipede into
pitcher.
2. Cover with screening or cheesecloth.

Look closely and see how each little segment of the millipede has two pairs of legs.

INSECTS

KITCHENWARE

SPIDER HOUSE

What You Need

milk carton
sticky plastic wrap
food (flies, bread crumbs, drops
of water for a drink)
spider

What to Do

1. Cut window out of milk carton.
2. Cover window with plastic wrap.
3. Add food and spider.

Watch the spider spin a web.

KITCHENWARE

Did you ever get completely absorbed in a job you wanted to do? Isn't it almost as if nothing else were important—time, eating, other people? This intense absorption in what *you* want to do is not much different with children when *they* want to do something. This is something all of us might care to remember.

Try this, for example, so you can see what I mean:

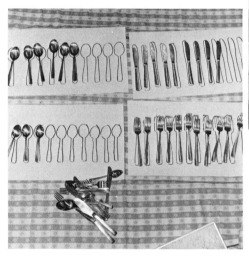

Someday, get out your dishes or silverware, scramble them all up, and ask your child to sort them all out. Then

- Watch to see how your child gets immersed in the job.
- See how different possibilities are considered.
- See a false start and what is done about it.
- See how the child forges ahead (not wanting to be interrupted) until the job is done and there is that victorious outburst *"I DID IT ! I DID IT !"*

Is a further reward needed?

MUSICAL INSTRUMENTS

Did you ever stop to think about why most children seem to like the kitchen more than any other room in the house (not counting that the food is there, of course)? It may well be because there are less "don't-touch things" in it than in any other room.

For example, see all those marvelous pots and pans,
    all kinds of spoons
        metal spoons,
        wooden spoons,
        jiggly measuring spoons

and dozens of other assorted things that make glorious sounds for marching, dancing, or just listening to.

This is not to say that there aren't other valuable things about the house—like combs (for example), from which you can make a kazoo. Do you know what a kazoo is? You wrap a piece of wax paper around the teeth of a comb and hum into it. It makes a zzzzzzzzz sound that tickles. Try it and you'll see.

WASHBOARD MUSIC. Run the head of a wooden clothespin up and down the ridges of a washboard. Also, try with thimbles on your fingers.

POT DRUM. Bang aluminum pot with a spoon or a stick.

POT-COVER CYMBALS. Strike two pot covers together.

POT-COVER GONG. Hold the pot cover by its handle and strike the edges of the cover with a stick.

NAIL BELLS. Jingle a handful of nails by cupping your two hands.

SPOON BELLS. Strike two spoons together.

WOODEN SPOONS RHYTHM STICKS. Hit two wooden mixing spoons together.

FORK TRIANGLE. Suspend a fork by a string. Strike with another fork.

MEASURING-SPOONS TAMBOURINE. Shake a set of measuring spoons.

SHOE-POLISH-CAN RATTLE. Put some peas, beans, rice, or small stones in an empty shoe-polish can. Shake.

CARDBOARD-TUBE HORN. Use any cardboard tube (toilet tissue, wax paper, etc). Sing, blow, or hum into one end. Cover or uncover other end with hand to make a variety of sounds.

OATMEAL-BOX DRUM. Take lid off oatmeal box. Punch holes on opposite sides of the box. Put string through the holes and tie the ends together. Put lid back on box and hang box around neck for playing.

PLASTIC-BOTTLE RATTLE. Put some beans, rice, or small stones in a plastic bottle. Close and shake.

TOILET-TISSUE-TUBE RATTLE. Cover one end of a toilet-tissue tube by pasting on some paper. Put beans or small stones inside. Cover other end of tube. Shake.

POTATO GRATER-SCRAPER. Scrape plastic grater with thimble, fork, or spoon.

SALT-BOX RATTLE. Use a salt box that still has salt in it. Tape over the opening. Shake box and the salt inside acts as a rattle.

PAPER-BAG RATTLE. Put some stones or beans into a small paper bag. Blow air into the bag and close with string or a rubber band. Shake.

KEY BELLS. Jingle keys from a key ring.

SANDPAPER BLOCKS. Glue or thumbtack two pieces of sandpaper to two blocks of wood. Rub together.

MONEY TAMBOURINE. Shake three coins by cupping your two hands.

MUSICAL INSTRUMENTS

57

PANTOMIME

Do you remember Charlie Chaplin of the old silent films? With no spoken words—with only a gesture and a flick of the eyebrow—what marvelous stories he could tell. Let your child be a pantomimist too. It's a delightful way to develop one's self-confidence and creativity.

WHAT WORK DO I DO?

- traffic cop
- house painter
- carpenter
- teacher
- violinist
- mailman
- shoemaker
- mother nursing baby
- bus driver
- boxer

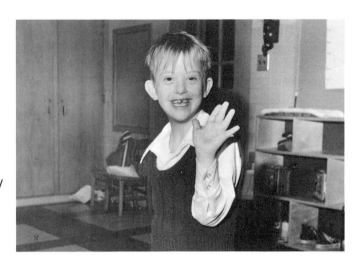

SHOW ME HOW YOU FEEL

- when your dog got run over
- when you go to bed at night
- when you go shopping with mother and get lost
- when it is very cold outside
- when your stomach hurts
- when a big dog jumps on you
- when someone takes away your ice-cream cone
- when you came in the room and you didn't expect to have a birthday party
- when the sun is shining

THINGS YOU DO WITH YOUR HANDS OR FINGERS

- *Sh . . . sh . . . sh . . . sh . . .*
- Stop.
- Come along.
- Scold someone.
- Wave goodbye.
- Thread a needle.
- Brush your teeth.
- Clean dirt from nail.
- Get something out of your tooth.
- Knock on the door.
- Make peace sign.

DIFFERENT WAYS OF WALKING

- Walk as if you were a model.
- Walk as if you were a soldier.
- Walk as if you were drunk.
- Walk as if you were very old.
- Walk as if you were a slowpoke.
- Walk as if you were a showoff.
- Walk as if you were in a big hurry.
- Walk as if your shoes hurt you.
- Walk as if you were proud of yourself.

WHAT HOUSEWORK AM I DOING?

- sweeping the floor
- dusting the furniture
- washing the dishes
- vacuuming
- setting the table
- hanging up the clothes
- raking leaves
- hosing the garden

WHAT AM I DOING?

- trying on a new hat
- reading the newspaper
- peeling a banana
- smelling perfume
- petting a kitten
- dialing a telephone number
- polishing shoes
- walking the dog

PARTS OF THE BODY

- Show me how your chest says, "I'm proud."
- Show me how your back says, "I'm an old, old man."
- Show me how your finger says, "Come here."
- Show me how your head says, "No !"
- Show me how your mouth says, "Mmm, I like that cookie."
- Show me how you use your ear to say, *"Sh,* do you hear the bird?"
- Show me what you do with your nose when there is a bad smell.

WHAT SPORT AM I PLAYING?

- bowling
- weight lifting
- swimming
- golfing
- rowing
- pitching ball
- wrestling
- jogging

PAPER

What fun it is to scribble—beautiful, free, uncontrolled scribbling.
No one to tell you how to "improve." No one to ask, "What is it?"
No one to direct, "Make it just like mine."

You can scribble on the floor.

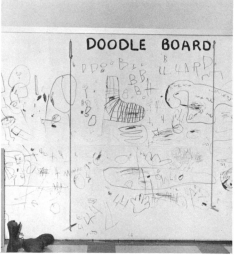

You can scribble on the wall.

You can scribble at the table.

You can scribble on a blackboard. If you don't have a blackboard, scribble on old newspaper or used wrapping paper.

PAPER

From all the squiggles and scribbles (it seems sometimes to adults that it will never end) at last comes a recognizable object—*ME !*

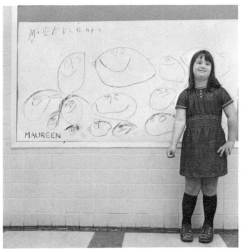

The pure refreshing glow of *"I did this —it's all mine !"*

Most children paint with the traditional poster paints—and, of course, that's fine. But wouldn't it be interesting to see what happens when you paint with

- muddy water
- berry juice
- coffee or tea
- corn syrup

What else can you think of?

Nor do you necessarily need to paint with a brush. See what effects you can get with

- fingertips
- pieces of sponge
- toothpicks
- house paint brushes
- felt-tip pens
- twigs
- rags

PAPER

Can you paint with a feather?

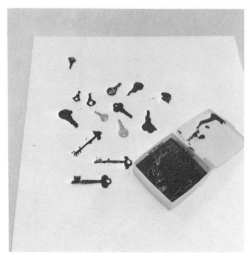

"Stamp and press . . . stamp and press." How children love to do print ! And it's so easy. Just take a few layers of paper toweling and soak them with paint. Then stamp with

- spools
- buttons
- a toilet-tissue roll
- a slice of carrot

What else is about that might be interesting to use?

A variety of materials to work on gives new problems—and makes one think creatively. Have you ever tried to paint or drawn on

- paper toweling
- newspaper
- stones
- wood
- fences
- cloth
- the sidewalk

PAPER If you work on a round base (or a square or a triangle), it sets up limits and makes you think differently about what you are going to do.

"This is where I live."

64

"Please don't help me. . . .
  Let me paint the way I want to. . . .
    Even if you don't like it—it's all right with me.
      When you keep wanting to help me,
        I begin to think, 'I can't do anything right.'
        In a little while, I start to believe it. . . .
          It makes me feel so bad inside,
            I just feel like giving up,
              AND THEN IT'LL BE TOO LATE TO BE ME ANY MORE."

"Masterpieces" for all to admire can
be suspended in a clothespin gallery.

PAPER

The aim of a mural (too big a job for one person) is not so much to be an artistic creation as it is to be one more planned experience to learn to work and play together cooperatively.

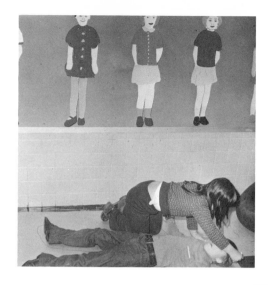

Did you ever see children's drawings with arms coming off the head or with the necks left out? Tracing the body helps a child "see" himself or herself realistically.

You can make a silhouette action mural if the body is traced in an action position, painted black, cut out—and then pasted on a large sheet of paper or a wall.

PAPER

A three-way mirror lets a child see and draw what she looks like from different angles.

"This is my hand."

A lot of "little hands" (and big ones of Mom and Dad too) on a large sheet of paper make an attractive and memorable wall hanging.

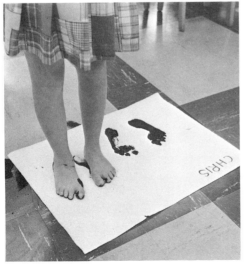

Of course, you can do the same thing with your feet.

68

How lucky for us that wallpaper books go out of date and we can get them "for nothing"—big sturdy sheets, the backs of which can be used for drawing on and the fronts for making "matching" games.

It is hard to say what there is about ripping and tearing that children enjoy. (Is it the *zzzzzzz* sound they make?)

If a child is given a stack of unwanted newspapers or magazines "just for ripping," you may find your child less destructive with valuable things about the house.

Demolishing a big piece of paper by punching holes with a wooden spoon is a tremendously absorbing activity for a child and is usually done with great abandon. But watch—someday those random holes may form an interesting pattern !

A child may not know "how to read" yet, but may enjoy "reading" the newspaper nevertheless.

- How many "e"s can you find? Cut them out.
- Hunt for the number "8." Put a big red ring around all the ones you find.
- Make a "Junior Shopping List" and find the breakfast foods you would like to buy.
- Find your favorite comic, cut it into sections, scramble the parts, and put them together again as they were.
- Find pictures of "helpers" in the community (like firemen), animals, various ethnic groups, well-known persons, means of transportation (like airplanes), various kinds of buildings, etc. Scrapbooks can be made from each of the categories.

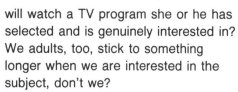

will watch a TV program she or he has selected and is genuinely interested in? We adults, too, stick to something longer when we are interested in the subject, don't we?

And so it is when we want a child to learn something special. Make a game of it and see how the attention span expands !

There are literally hundreds of commercially manufactured "number" games, but an improvised homemade one can have much more appeal. Try this target game with an "instant" ball made from a squashed piece of newspaper tied with a string or rubber band.

Have you ever noticed how long (sometimes an hour or more) a child

Snakes (children love dramatic names for games) is just sheets of paper with numbers. Scores can be added up or not added up, as desired.

PAPER

The same paper sheets can be rearranged to play Elephants. Whichever way, there are numbers that can be introduced, making the excitement of learning possible.

A domino game helps find "likenesses" and "differences."

PAPER

PLANTS

Isn't it interesting to know that people will not connect these dots in the same way?

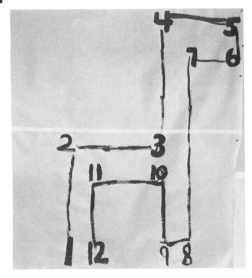

If you follow the numbers, you get a little "number-work" interest. This happens to be a giraffe, but you can also make a snake, a house, a person —what about the "biggest mountain in the world"?

PLANTS

"If you want me to learn something,
Please let me go slow. . . .
Let me look at things. . . .
Let me touch and handle things. . . .
Let me hear . . .
And smell . . .
And maybe taste things.
Oh, how many things I can
Find out by myself
If you let me go slow—please !"

It's a little harder to find vacant lots nowadays, but if you walk to the corner, go around the block, look behind the school (even if you look in cracks of sidewalks) and look carefully—you may be rewarded with some of the most spectacular treasures of the world. Some in the spring, some in the summer, some in the autumn, and some standing undaunted above the snow.

- brilliant yellow buttercups waiting to be placed under chins for the "do you like butter?" test
- milkweed, with its skeins of floss, shining like pearls floating through the air
- cattails
- prickly thistle
- sweet clover (Did you ever find a four-leaf clover?)
- the intricate patterns of Queen Anne's lace
- indomitable dandelions with their seeds sailing off in the wind
- horse chestnuts—just right to be stored in the pockets of little boys and girls to use as "money"
- yellow, orange, and scarlet leaves following the slightest breeze as they fall to the ground—in autumn when their work is done
- chicory

Do you see the winter buds all ready with their tiny beginnings of next year's twigs?

Did you ever make a set of "cups and saucers" from the acorns of the oak tree?

74

"DON'T TOUCH !" Such a sad order for a child who loves to
touch and who needs so many free, unthreatened chances to pile
up exciting *feeling* sensations like

- playing in rain puddles
- jumping on a pile of leaves
- prickly pine needles
- rolling down a hill
- bark
- feathers
- icicles
- a caterpillar going up one's arm—or a ladybug

What a rich exciting collection of *smells* can be collected in early
childhood—some, oh, so pleasant; some awful—but each telling
a little more about the world around us and staying forever (or at
least for a long time) with us.

- Did you ever smell grass after a rain?
- Did you ever smell grass after it was just cut?
- Do all flowers smell the same? Do you think you will ever forget the first time you smelled apple blossoms?
- Did you ever smell smoke at a campfire?
- Did you ever smell
  - new shoes?
  - a barnyard?
  - the ocean?
  - a baby after a bath?
  - a candy factory?
- Did you ever smell bread from an oven?

Some people consider grass and daisies "just common." But if *you* like their pretty flowers and if *you* think they are something very special, your child almost surely will too. A few moments of wonder and discovery—added up—can help form a sensitivity to nature that will enrich a life beyond measure.

Aren't these dry wildflowers (picked ever so gently so you don't pull out their precious roots !) a gay sight in these little vases made from the children's wooden beads?

MAKE YOUR OWN PERFUME

What You Need

    petals (rose, lily-of-the-valley, lilac)
    jar with lid or cork

What to Do

1. Pick petals of flowers that have a pretty fragrance.
2. Let petals dry for a couple of days.
3. Put petals in jar.
4. Cover jar with lid or cork.

MY FLOWER BOOK

DAISY

Queen Anne's Lace

David
August 27

A wildflower notebook can be very precious to a child. Why shouldn't it be, since every flower represents a joyful outdoor discovery? Are there misspellings in the notebook? Poor grammar? Sloppy writing? No matter—this notebook is the child's and not an object for adult judgments.

OAK LEAF

SEPTEMBER 9

Most trees are too high for little children. But when their leaves and seeds (in all their elegant autumn tints) flutter to the ground, and are mounted into leaf and/or seed notebooks, a child has first lessons in observation and classification. Science is then a joy—*not* "drudgery."

How many different leaves can be found near your house? Going around the block? On the way to school?

When you put acorns on your fingertips, they become hats for finger puppets.

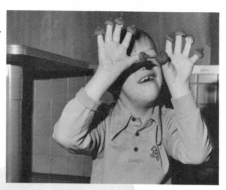

MY SEED BOOK

MAPLE SEEDS

JAMES BUELL

A crown of maple leaves is a very special crown for a child. Have you ever made a crown from long-stemmed daisies? or Queen Anne's lace? They are also very appropriate for "playing wedding."

Sycamore leaves are so big and so pretty, you can put them up on your wall (like a mural) to look at in the wintertime when it is cold and blustery outside.

Sycamore leaves are often big enough to use as a mat for your dinner plate.

Every single name in the world can be
written with twigs. Twigs are also good
for practicing addresses, phone
numbers, ages, etc.

A bulb store is good for number
practice, "please and thank-you"
practice—and to beautify the
neighborhood. Of course, you can also
have a seed store.

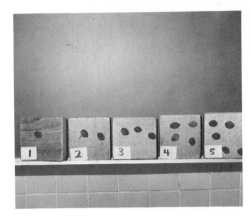

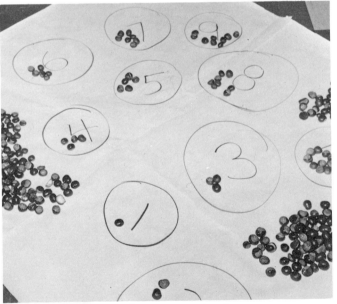

Do you have peach stones, Chinese lanterns, or chestnuts about? Why not use some of them for learning? They can help make abstract concepts come alive for a child.

I dropped a seed into the earth.
It grew, and the plant was mine.

It was a wonderful thing, this plant of mine.
I did not know its name.
All I know is that I planted something apparently as lifeless
        as a grain of sand.
And there came forth a green and living thing
        unlike the seed,
        unlike the soil in which it stood,
        unlike the air into which it grew.

No one could tell me why it grew, or how.
It has secrets all its own, secrets that baffle the wisest men.

Yet, this plant was my friend.

It faded when I withheld the light,
        It wilted when I neglected to give it water,
            It flourished when I supplied its simple needs.

One week I went away on a vacation, and when I returned the plant was
        dead, and I missed it.

Although my little plant had died so soon, it had taught me a lesson.
The lesson is that it is worthwhile to have a plant.*

*From *The Nature-Study Idea,* by L.H. Bailey

STRING BEANS

APRIL 26

One of the best reasons for indoor gardening for a child is that so many of the projects give almost instant results.

Some plants pop up in just two or three days. Such things as an avocado seed take longer.

But watch the thrill that comes when the seed finally does split open and your child sees the first signs of life !

So gather up the orange and grapefruit seeds from your morning's breakfast, cut down the used milk cartons, AND MAKE A CONSERVATORY ON YOUR WINDOW SILLS.

84

SEED SPONGE

What You Need

> seeds (grass, clover, mustard, etc.)
> sponge
> plastic bag
> string

What to Do

1. Wet the sponge.
2. Put seeds in holes of sponge.
3. Put sponge in plastic bag till seeds germinate.
4. Attach string and suspend by window.

GRASS-SEED GARDEN

What You Need

> grass seed
> sponge

What to Do

1. Wet the sponge.
2. Roll sponge in grass seed.
3. Place in saucer.

In a few days the sponge will be covered with grass.

A STRANGE GARDEN

What You Need

> slice of bread
> 2 saucers
> water

What to Do

1. Put bread in saucer.
2. Wait about an hour.
3. Cover bread with other saucer.
4. Add a few drops of water from time to time.

After a few days, look at the mold (fine threads with black specks).

TERRARIUM

What You Need

plants you like (with roots)
glass bowl
sticky plastic wrap or aluminum foil
soil and stones

What to Do

1. Put stones on bottom of bowl.
2. Add soil and plants.
3. Sprinkle with water.
4. Cover with plastic wrap or foil.

Add twigs, stones, or shells for more interest.

WATERMELON GARDEN (pumpkin, squash)

What You Need

watermelon, pumpkin, or squash seeds
drinking glass
paper towel
water

What to Do

1. Line inside of glass with wet paper towel.
2. Place seeds between the glass and towel.
3. Leave an inch of water at the bottom.

Watch the roots grow.

PLANTS

CLIMBING BEAN VINE

What You Need

a few bean seeds   stick for trellis
milk carton   soil

What to Do

1. Cut off top of milk carton.
2. Add soil.
3. Put beans in soil.
4. Cover with about ½ inch of soil.
5. Keep moist.
6. Put on sunny window sill.
7. Use trellis when vine forms.

HOW TO START A NEW PLANT

What You Need

    plant (geranium, ivy, etc.)
    jar
    knife
    water

What to Do

1. Using a knife, cut (on a slant) about 6 inches off the tip of plant. Be sure you have three or four leaves on it.
2. Place in jar of water.
3. Place on sunny window sill and watch roots form.

HOW PLANTS GET THEIR FOOD

What You Need

    celery stalks
    drinking glass
    water
    red food coloring

What to Do

1. Add a few drops of food coloring to ½ glass of water.
2. Place celery in water.
3. Leave overnight.

Watch the long red tubes.

Do the same with grass, maple, oak, and chestnut leaves.

FORCING BRANCHES

What You Need

    branches of forsythia, pussy willow, and trees
    like apple, cherry, peach, and maple
    tall jar

What to Do

1. As it gets close to spring, cut branches with lots of buds.
2. Place in jar of warm water.

Forsythia will open in five to ten days.

Use as a centerpiece at dinner table.

FRUIT ORCHARD

What You Need

seeds (apple, grapefruit, orange, lemon)
soil
box

What to Do

1. Put soil in box.
2. Add seeds in a row.
3. Cover with ¼ inch soil.
4. Keep moist.
5. Place near sunny window.

LENTIL GARDEN

What You Need

lentil seeds
soup bowl
water

What to Do

1. Put water in bowl.
2. Put lentil seeds in water.
3. Set in warm dark place.
4. When leaves start to grow, bring bowl to window.

PLANTS

POPCORN GARDEN

What You Need

unpopped popcorn
glass
soil
water

What to Do

1. Put soil in glass.
2. Push seeds down alongside of glass so that they will show.
3. Keep soil moist.

Watch seeds sprout in a few days.

MUFFIN-TIN HERB GARDEN

What You Need

    herb seeds (sage, thyme, basil, rosemary, chives)
    muffin tin
    soil

What to Do

1. Put soil in sections of muffin tin.
2. Add seeds.
3. Cover lightly with soil.
4. Keep moist.

Cut leaves with scissors and add to salads, soups, and sandwiches.

GARLIC PLANT

What You Need

    garlic
    soil
    can

What to Do

1. Remove two or three cloves from garlic (do not take peel off garlic).
2. Put soil in can.
3. Add garlic cloves (tips upward).
4. Keep moist.

Snip off bits of plant as needed for flavoring of soups or salads.

POTATO PLANT

What You Need

    potato
    cup
    soil
    water

What to Do

1. Keep potato in a dark, warm place until an eye has sprouted a couple of inches.
2. Cut out the piece that has the sprouted eye.
3. Put soil in cup (about 2 inches) and plant the sprout.
4. Keep soil damp.

PINEAPPLE PLANT

What You Need

pineapple
dish
stones
water

What to Do

1. Cut off top of pineapple (leaves) and about one inch of fruit.
2. Put in a dish.
3. Fill dish with stones.
4. Cover stones with water.
5. Keep near sunny window.

Watch leaves and roots form in a few weeks.
Then transplant into pot with soil.

ONION PLANT

What You Need

onion
dish
stones
water

What to Do

1. Put onion in dish of small stones.
2. Add water.
3. Put in warm dark place.
4. Bring to light after it grows a couple of inches.

DRAW A BRANCH

What You Need

branch (with no leaves on)
vase
pencil, crayons, or paint

What to Do

1. Put branch in vase.
2. Look at branch carefully and draw it.

GRASS AND SEED-POD ARRANGEMENT

What You Need

dried grasses and seed pods
can
Styrofoam or clay

What to Do

1. Put Styrofoam or clay on bottom of can.
2. Set grasses and seed pods inside.

LEAF MOBILE

What You Need

thread
glue
assorted leaves
coat hanger

What to Do

1. Cut threads of different lengths.
2. Glue leaves to threads.
3. Tie threads to coat hanger and suspend.

PLANTS

PLASTIC

Ask neighbors and neighborhood stores to save those plastic blocks used for packing appliances. These blocks can build just about anything wooden blocks can and, at the same time, have one special advantage: they are easier on parents' ears !

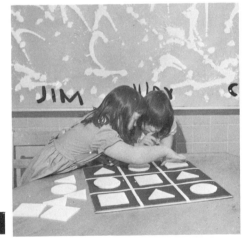

Sheetlike plastic pieces can be made into lotto games, such as this one for "matching shapes." Color the pieces and you can make a "color lotto" game.

If you can get two of the same sample ceramic-tile sets, you can make another fine "match the color" lotto game.

Watch little Michelle. Her determined spirit is not much different from that of an architect at a drawing board.

92

Discarded plastic-tile samples can be used for a sturdy "number matching" game.

"Look what I can do with my mouth!" A child doesn't need detailed scientific information for the "whys" of this phenomenon. Just to see and wonder is enough for now.

- You might care to purchase an inexpensive magnifying glass for a birthday present.
- If you have a magnet, let your child use it.
- Let your child see what happens when a thermometer is placed in the sun, the shade, or hot water.
- What dissolves in water? Sugar? Pebbles? What floats?

PLASTIC

A "plastic-things" collage helps to dramatize plastic as a "material." Other collages can be made of paper, wood, metal, etc.

PUPPETS

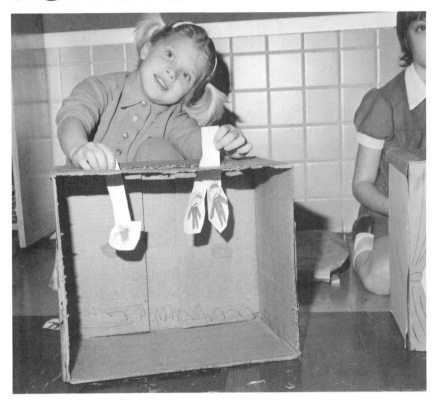

Puppets are little jiggly people that can be made from just about anything:

- a fingertip
- an old rubber ball
- a sock

Do you know that you can make a dragon from a carrot?

Yes ! A very fine dragon indeed !

Also, puppets can be anything or anybody on earth (or in the whole universe). He or she can be

- A worker in an assembly line
- An astronaut
- A clown
- A ballerina
- A sea lion
- A robot

If you have lost a mitten, why not make an "instant" puppet from the one you have left?

94

ACORN PUPPETS

Place acorns (hats) on fingertips.
Draw faces on fingers.

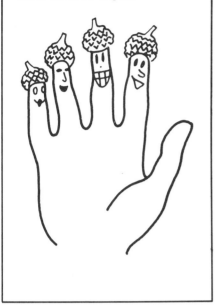

PALM PUPPETS

Draw face on palm of hand.
Be sure to draw eyes on one of the
palm lines so that the wrinkle will look
like eyes closing when the hand closes.

THUMB AND INDEX-FINGER PUPPET

Draw face (with lips on thumb and index
finger).
Manipulate thumb.

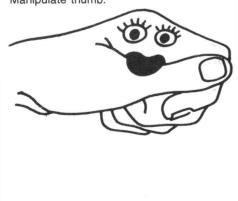

FINGER-RING PUPPETS

Make faces from paper or cardboard.
Attach to elastic or paper band to fit
fingers.

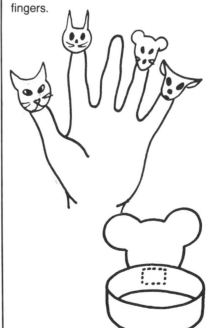

TINY BAG PUPPET

Draw a face on a tiny paper bag.
Cut a hole for a finger nose.
Your thumb and middle finger become arms.

PAPER-PLATE PUPPET

Draw a face on paper plate.
Attach stick to back of plate with tape or thumbtacks.

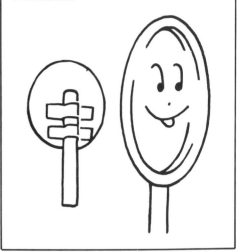

PAPER-BAG PUPPET

Draw a face on the bottom of the bag, placing part of the mouth on lower edge. Continue inside of mouth on fold and onto the side of the bag.

STUFFED PAPER-BAG PUPPET

Stuff a paper bag with newspaper.
Slip a stick or paper-towel roll into the paper bag.
Tie the bag at the neck with string or use a rubber band.

BALL PUPPET

Make a hole in the ball (tennis, rubber, or Styrofoam) the size of finger.
Glue buttons for eyes, yarn for hair, etc. Or use felt-tip marker.
Push a handkerchief into the hole with finger.

PATTERN PUPPET

Cut out two pieces of cloth, as in this drawing.
Sew together, leaving an opening for the hand.
Draw in face and add buttons.

STICK PUPPET

Find a magazine picture of someone standing up.
Paste onto cardboard and cut out.
Attach to stick or ruler with masking tape.

NYLON-STOCKING PUPPET

Stuff toe of stocking with rags.
Add a stick to the toe.
Use a rubber band or string for the neck.

PUPPETS

SOCK PUPPET

Fill a sock with rags.
Stick a ruler into sock.
Keep secure with a rubber band or string.

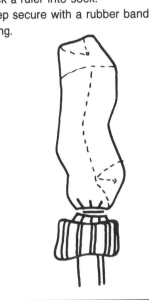

SOCK PUPPET

Stuff bottom of sock.
Tie heel and toe with string or rubber band.
Insert ruler into heel.

SPOOL OR DARNING-THREAD PUPPET

Insert stick or rod through hole of spool.
Cover with handkerchief.
Tie with string or use rubber band at neck.

CLOTHES PIN PUPPET

Draw face and clothing on clothes pin or use scraps of cloth for clothing.

TUBE PUPPET

Use a toilet-tissue tube for the body and a popsicle stick (with tape inside) for handle.
Draw a face if you wish.

FINGER PUPPET

Draw a head or cut one out from a magazine.
Paste head onto cardboard and cut it out.
Attach to finger with string or rubber band.

PICTURE PUPPET

Draw a character or cut one out from a magazine.
Paste picture onto cardboard.
Attach to tongue depressor with masking tape, thumbtack, or stapler.

THUMB PUPPET

Wrap a handkerchief around hand and four fingers, excluding the thumb.
Draw a face on thumb.

WOODEN-SPOON PUPPET

Put on a face.

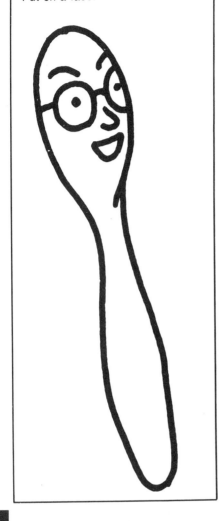

WINDOW STAGE

Puppets can be worked on a window sill.

Or put a cloth across the window.
Work puppets from behind cloth.

BOX STAGE

Cut out back and front of box.
Put on table.

TWO-BOX STAGE

Set two boxes on top of each other. Have the side of one open for viewing. Cut out slot so that puppet can be worked from the bottom.

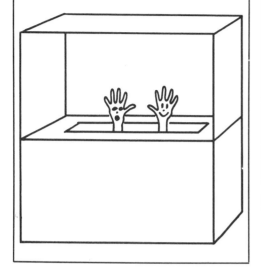

DOORWAY STAGE

Attach sheet, curtain, or blanket to doorway.

POST OR TREE STAGE

Tie rope to two posts or trees. Suspend sheet, curtain, or blanket from rope.

BIG CARTON STAGE

Remove one side of carton.
Cut out hole for stage.
Set on floor.

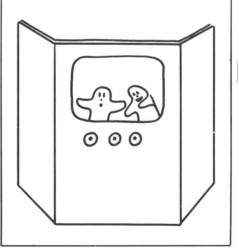

PUPPETS

TABLE STAGE

Have table in usual upright position. Cover one side with sheet, blanket, or large towel.

ANOTHER TABLE STAGE

Turn table on its side.

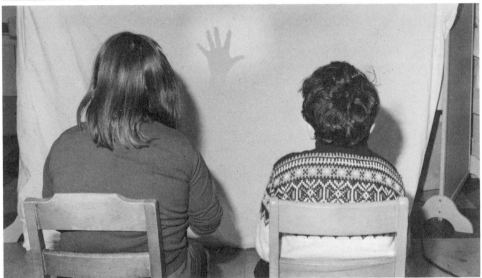

SHADOW THEATER

It takes just a couple of minutes to set up a shadow theater. Tie a sheet across a doorway or some kind of posts. Put a bare light *behind* the object you want silhouetted. This will cast a shadow on the sheet.

- Stick two fingers up and you will have a rabbit's head.
- Hold out your arm and two fingers and you will have a crocodile that can open and close its mouth.
- If you go far away from the sheet, you can be an elf. If you go close to the sheet, you can be a giant.
- Do you want to have a boxing match? Get a friend and shadow-box with each other. (But you must make sure to moan and groan at the right time !)

Fairy Tales for Puppets

Fathers, mothers, grandparents, and (yes !) great-grandparents would gladly admit to their having gone through the "fairy-tale stage" —and onward, perhaps to the highest ranks of science, mathematics, and philosophy.

You can find all these generations-old, tell-me-again stories in libraries. They can be read for pleasure and/or reread with the idea of making up a puppet play. It really won't be necessary to memorize parts. Just watch how the children will make up the parts as they go along.

THE THREE BEARS

CINDERELLA

JACK AND THE BEANSTALK

PETER RABBIT

RUMPELSTILTSKIN

THE PRINCESS AND THE PEA

THE EMPEROR'S NEW CLOTHES

SLEEPING BEAUTY

SNOW WHITE AND THE SEVEN DWARFS

THE UGLY DUCKLING

HENNY PENNY

HANSEL AND GRETEL

THE GINGERBREAD BOY

LITTLE RED RIDING HOOD

THE ELVES AND THE SHOEMAKER

TOM THUMB

PINOCCHIO

THE LITTLE RED HEN AND THE GRAIN OF WHEAT

THREE BILLY GOATS GRUFF

SNOW WHITE AND ROSE RED

PUPPETS

Aesop's Fables for Puppets

The combination of Aesop's fables and lively puppets is made to order for moral training.

Of course, we know that animals don't talk the way we do, but Aesop, a wise old man who lived over twenty-five hundred years ago, tried to teach "lessons" by using animals.

For example, when he wanted to talk about a king's cruelty to a slave, he wrote about a lion (instead of a king).

THE BOY AND THE NUTS

MORAL: Don't be greedy.

BOY: Mother, may I have some nuts?
MOTHER: Yes, Son. *(Boy puts hand in jar and grabs a whole fistful of nuts.)*
BOY: Oh, Mother, Mother. I can't get my hand out ! *(Boy pulls and pulls, but can't get his hand out.)*
MOTHER: Let some of the nuts go. Then you will be able to get your hand through.
BOY: No ! No ! I want all the nuts. What a mean old jar ! *(Cries.)*
MOTHER: No, Son. It's not the jar's fault. If you take so many nuts at one time, you won't be able to get your hand out. If you were not greedy and just took a few at a time, you could get your hand out with no trouble at all.

THE GRASSHOPPER AND THE ANTS

MORAL: You can't play all the time; sometimes you have to work.

ANT: *Drags along a big chunk of food.*
GRASSHOPPER: Oh, I'm so hungry. Can I have some of your food?
ANT: Why do you come to me for food? What were you doing all summer?
GRASSHOPPER: Oh, I had such a wonderful time. I sang and sang and sang—all the time.
ANT: I worked and I worked and I worked—all the time. Now I have lots of food for the winter. Too bad for you. Now you will have to go without food.

THE SHEPHERD AND THE WOLF

MORAL: If you lie, people will not believe you when you tell the truth.

The SHEPHERD BOY *wants to play a joke on the village people while he is watching the sheep.*

SHEPHERD BOY: Wolf ! Wolf !
Village people run in to help.
PEOPLE: There is no wolf here. Let us go back.
They go back.
SHEPHERD BOY: Wolf ! Wolf !
Village people run in to help.
PEOPLE : There is no wolf here. Let us go back. *(They go back.)*
A real wolf comes and attacks sheep.
SHEPHERD BOY: Wolf ! Wolf ! Wolf ! Wolf !
The village people do not come.

THE CAT AND THE MICE

MORAL: It's easy to think of a plan. But can you carry the plan out?

MOUSE 1: That cat worries me.
MOUSE 2: That cat worries me too.
MOUSE 1: What do you think we can do about it?
MOUSE 2: Let's tie a bell around her neck. Then we will know when she is coming. Then we can all run home.
MOUSE 1: Yes, that's a great idea.
MOUSE 2: It's a great idea all right. But which one of us will put the bell around the cat's neck?

THE MILKMAID AND HER PAIL

MORAL: Don't count your chickens before they're hatched.

MILKMAID: *Carries a pail of milk on her head and dreams about what she will do with the money she will make when she sells it.*
MILKMAID: I shall churn the milk into butter.
Then I shall sell the butter and buy some eggs.
The eggs will hatch and I will have some chicks.
When the chicks are a good size, I shall sell them.
With the money, I shall buy a new dress. And all the boys will fall in love with me. But I shall say, "Pooh ! Pooh !"

As the milkmaid says this, she tosses her head, and the pail of milk falls to the ground.

Pretend Stories for Puppets

Puppets can make self-conscious children forget themselves, limber up a bit, and start to chatter away with little or no inhibition.

Tensions that could have built up into explosions can be headed off by puppets. (A little "puppet therapy"—I see it so often and yet cannot explain the "why" of it.)

Try a spur-of-the-moment story and see what happens at these places:

- AT THE LAUNDROMAT
- ON A RAFT
- WAITING FOR A BUS
- AT THE DENTIST'S OFFICE
- AT THE NORTH POLE
- ON TOP OF A MOUNTAIN
- IN A CAVE
- RIDING A CAMEL
- IN AN ELEVATOR
- AT THE CHECK-OUT COUNTER
- AT THE ZOO
- IN A SUBMARINE
- ON THE ESCALATOR
- SITTING ON THE PORCH
- IN A HELICOPTER
- AT THE BARBERSHOP
- IN A LIGHTHOUSE
- IN A LITTLE FAR-OFF VILLAGE
- AT THE ROAD STAND
- AT AN AUCTION SALE

Jokes for Puppets

Just about everybody has a funny bone. You might care to try having some lively puppet tickle it with some of these familiar silly jokes.

PUPPET 1: If an apple a day keeps the doctor away, what does an onion do?
PUPPET 2: Keeps everyone away.

* * *

PUPPET 1: Do you file your nails?
PUPPET 2: No. I just cut them off and throw them away.

* * *

PUPPET 1: What is the best way to get to the hospital?
PUPPET 2: Stand in the middle of traffic.

* * *

PUPPET 1: Why did Miss Muffet need a road map?
PUPPET 2: Because she lost her whey (way).

* * *

PUPPET 1: Do you like homework?
PUPPET 2: I like "nothing" better.

* * *

PUPPET 1: If a fly got caught in a pitcher of honey, how would it get out?
PUPPET 2: I don't know. I'm stuck.
PUPPET 1: So's the fly !

* * *

PUPPET 1: *Cries loudly.*
PUPPET 2: Why are you crying?
PUPPET 1: I lost my dog.
PUPPET 2: Did you put a "lost dog" ad in the paper?
PUPPET 1: No. It wouldn't do any good. My dog can't read.

PUPPET 1: What's the hardest thing about learning to roller skate?
PUPPET 2: The floor.

* * *

PUPPET 1: Use the word "tackle" in a sentence.
PUPPET 2: Anyone who sits on a "tackle" (tack will) be sorry.

* * *

PUPPET 1: You have a nice dog. What's her name?
PUPPET 2: Ginger.
PUPPET 1: What does Ginger do?
PUPPET 2: Ginger snaps.

* * *

PUPPET 1: Did you ever hear of the rope joke?
PUPPET 2: No.
PUPPET 1: Skip it.

* * *

PUPPET 1: (SALESMAN) Good morning. Can I help you?
PUPPET 2: I would like to buy a puppy.
PUPPET 1: Good.
PUPPET 2: How much are they?
PUPPET 1: Ten dollars apiece.
PUPPET 2: I don't want to buy a piece of puppy. I want to buy a whole one.

* * *

PUPPET 1: Use the word "barrel" in a sentence.
PUPPET 2: Run or the "barrel" (bear will) bite you.

PUPPETS

107

Riddles for Puppets

There are some ageless riddles.

Some are so old, nobody knows who made them up !

Some are just for ordinary children who might be wrigglers.

Some are for those who are a little slow at "getting started."

Some for those who may be a little awkward.

Some are for those who are sometimes uncooperative and those who are sometimes overly aggressive.

And some are for all of those who just don't seem to fit into the general pattern of things and are a little bit apathetic about learning.

For these children, let their puppets tell riddles. Here are some favorites:

RIDDLE	ANSWER
What is the difference between an old dime and a new nickel?	Five cents.
Why does the chicken cross the road?	To get to the other side.
What do hippopotamuses have that no other animals have?	Little hippopotamuses.
What has four legs but only one foot?	A bed.
Why do birds fly south for the winter?	Because they can't walk.
When a boy falls into the water, what is the first thing he does?	He gets wet.
Two boys and a girl are under one umbrella but none of them gets wet. Why not?	It isn't raining.
The more you take away from me, the bigger I become. What am I?	A hole.
What is filled every morning and emptied every night?	A shoe.
How do you know the elephant will stay for a long time when he comes to visit?	He brings his trunk.
What is a kitten after it is four days old?	Five days old.
How long is a shoe?	1 foot long.
What letter can sting?	B (bee).

RIDDLE	ANSWER
When the clock strikes 13, what time is it?	Time to have the clock repaired.
Which flowers do you wear all year around?	Tulips (two lips).
What is it that is full of holes and yet holds water?	A sponge.
What has a face and hands but no body or legs?	A clock.
What travels all over and still stays in one corner?	A postage stamp.
What gets wetter as it dries?	A towel.
Why does a donkey go over the mountain?	Because he can't go under it.
What did the earth say when it rained?	"If this keeps up, my name is mud."
What did one wall say to the other wall?	"Meet you at the corner."
What did the carpet say to the floor?	"I've got you covered."
What is it that goes up and never goes down?	Your age.
What can be heard but never seen?	A song.
What is the longest word in the English language?	"Smiles." There is a mile between the first and last letter.
When do 2 and 2 make more than 4?	When they make 22.
What makes more noise than a pig stuck in a fence?	Two pigs stuck in a fence.
As I was going to St. Ives I met a man with seven wives. Each wife had seven sacks, Each sack had seven cats, Each cat had seven kits. Kits, cats, sacks, wives, How many were going to St. Ives?	Only one. The seven wives were going in the other direction.
Which animal cannot tell the truth?	Lion (lyin').
What has arms and legs but no head?	A chair.

PUPPETS

109

Nursery Rhymes for Puppets

Did you ever stop to think how terribly nonsensical some of the old nursery rhymes are? And yet their words and catchy rhythms, repeated over and over again, have made marks on people's minds that have lasted for generations.

Bouncy puppets have a special genius for acting out these nursery rhymes.

See how good the audience is at guessing which rhyme the puppet is doing:

HUMPTY DUMPTY

JACK BE NIMBLE

LITTLE JACK HORNER

JACK AND JILL

LITTLE BOY BLUE

LITTLE BO PEEP

DING-DONG BELL

BAA, BAA, BLACK SHEEP

SEESAW MARGERY DAW

MARY HAD A LITTLE LAMB

HEY DIDDLE DIDDLE

HICKORY DICKORY DOCK

SING A SONG OF SIXPENCE

LITTLE TOMMY TUCKER

JACK SPRAT COULD EAT NO FAT

DEEDLE, DEEDLE DUMPLING, MY SON, JOHN

SIMPLE SIMON

Teaching Lessons for Puppets

Even though puppets are mostly comedians, they do enjoy helping out parents and teachers who think children need to learn important "lessons."

See how a totally uninterested child will perk up and want to rush to brush his or her teeth just because "Jocko said to." Long-winded advice, bribes, or threats often cannot do as effective a job !

In addition, there are always those children who resent such questions from adults as "Did you wash your neck today?" A happy, lighthearted puppet could ask this question and receive a reasonable response !

Some lessons could include:

- "Don't be a litterbug."
- "Save energy."
- Treating your neighbor the way you want to be treated
- Helping at home
- Waiting your turn
- "Haste makes waste."
- Integration. Respect for differences
- The meaning of holidays
- Sex education
- Sharing
- Be kind to animals
- Martin Luther King
- Honesty
- Good Sportsmanship
- Courtesy

Folk Songs for Puppets

Puppets are superb directors for "sing-a-longs," especially if the song suggests some action. You see, puppets are amazingly versatile, being able to

row boats
ride ponies
or climb mountains, etc.

Try any one of these songs.

THE FARMER IN THE DELL

LONDON BRIDGE

ROW, ROW, ROW YOUR BOAT

SKIP TO MY LOU

OLD MACDONALD HAD A FARM

CLEMENTINE

FIDDLE DEE DEE

THE BLUE-TAIL FLY

HE'S GOT THE WHOLE WORLD IN HIS HANDS

FRÈRE JACQUES (ARE YOU SLEEPING?)

IF YOU'RE HAPPY AND YOU KNOW IT

SWEET BETSY FROM PIKE

SHE'LL BE COMIN' ROUND THE MOUNTAIN

ON TOP OF OLD SMOKY

YANKEE DOODLE

DOWN IN THE VALLEY

JIMMY CRACKED CORN

PAW PAW PATCH

BILLY BOY

GO ROUND AND ROUND THE VILLAGE

Don't forget that puppets are also good at leading rounds! "Are You Sleeping?" "Row, Row, Row Your Boat," etc.

Dancing for Puppets

Puppets are excellent dancers too.

Watch them whirl, leap, and fly through the air.

Notice, too, the magnificent sweeping grand bows they make when they are done.

You might consider having the dances synchronized with music tapes, the radio, or the record player.

Do you have any classical records? If you do, you're in luck, because many of them are wonderful for puppets to dance to.

(Here's a very special tip if you want some extra chuckles for your audience: play the record in slow motion !)

Here are some charming, dramatically easy-to-dance-to ones:

NUTCRACKER SUITE by Tschaikowsky

TOY SYMPHONY by Haydn

THE BUTTERFLY DANCE by Grieg

ANVIL CHORUS (from *Il Trovatore*) by Verdi

MARCH OF THE TOYS by Herbert

PARADE OF THE WOODEN SOLDIERS by Jessel

MARCHE MILITAIRE by Schubert

TOREADOR SONG (from *Carmen*) by Bizet

INVITATION TO THE DANCE by Weber

HALL OF THE MOUNTAIN KING by Grieg

FUNERAL MARCH OF A MARIONETTE by Gounod

ANITRA'S DANCE by Grieg

WALTZING DOLL by Saint-Saëns

SCARF DANCE by Chaminade

READING

Some Comments About
the Matter of Reading

My experience convinces me that most parents really do want their children to learn to read and that most children start school eager for this. Yet, somewhere along the line something at times goes wrong and interest starts to wane.

I am convinced that children can become interested in reading and want to learn to read when reading is important and relevant to their lives—*NOW.*

When you stop to think about it, children really aren't much different from us adults—when we *want* to do a thing, we usually can do it better and faster. Whether it is to learn to play the piano, learn a second language for a trip we are going to take, or learn to bake bread.

We know these things about ourselves, but sometimes when we deal with children, we forget and the motivation becomes *"DO IT BECAUSE IT'S GOOD FOR YOU !"*

Sometimes it is important for us to stop and ask ourselves:

- Do our children see that reading is important to our lives?
- Do they see that when we want to relax, we choose to pick up a book to read?
- Do they see us bringing along a book to read on the bus or the plane or when we have to wait at the dentist's office?
- Do they see us willingly look up a word in the dictionary? Or look up material in an encyclopedia?
- Do they see us going to the library, and do we take the children along with us?

- Do we have a special time (perhaps before bedtime) just for reading? Laps are wonderful for listening on, and so is sprawling out on the living-room floor—both ideal spots for squeezing in another "any old time" story during the day.

Any adult who wants to whet children's appetites and lure them to enjoy the printed word may deliberately spread open the newspaper and let the children see him or her enjoying the reading. Perhaps you could share discussion on important events:

the weather report,	some sports events,
the comics,	the advertisements, etc.

ATTITUDES CAN BE VERY CONTAGIOUS !

"Wait till you get to school!" Have you ever heard an adult say this to a child when he or she asks a question that has to do with reading? It can be very discouraging when a curious child is rebuffed this way. *Wanting to read* is a big chunk of the whole reading process. And this can be developed long before school starts.

Try a family newspaper. Even if a child does not know how to write, material can be dictated to you or an older sister or brother. The main thing is that the child "see" the importance of the printed word.

THE LEWIS FAMILY NEWSPAPER

| Sunny | MARCH | 1¢. cost |

Goldy (our goldfish) died on March 6. She was sick.

Mom and Dad are painting the house. It is green cblor

Aunt ELLa got a new car. It is a VW. It is red. She took us for a ride in it.

GRANDMA IS GOING TO NITL NIGHt SCHOOL! She is going to learn auto fixing so she can fix her car herself Hurray for GRANDMA!!

STAFF
Gloria Harris

News can include original favorite poems, jokes, songs, coming events, etc.

READING

MADISON MONTHLY NEWS
STREET

	DECEMBER	COST: FREE
The Jones family (24 Madison, rear) wishes to report that they got a new baby. Her name is Sharon. Sharon was born on December 7. She weighs 7 pounds. CONGRATULATIONS	KITTENS- HOME WANTED for 6 kittens born to the Lehman family. NO CHARGE	Ride Needed Mr. Roy Clark on 78 Madison (upper flat) is looking for someone who drives downtown daily — about 8:30 AM. Will pitch in for gas. Much apprecieated
GARAGE SALE The Burnetts on 40 Madison are having a big garage sale on Dec. 4 COME ONE- COME ALL. Everything cheep.	SPECial ! Anyone who wants to pitch in to buy tulips for the island on our street: Contact Mrs. Jennifer Baldwin 834-9178 (between 6-8 PM)	Editor JUDY MASON 18 Madison Street

You might want to encourage a monthly street newspaper like Judy's.

THE LEWIS FAMILY NEWSPAPER

Sunny ☀   MARCH   1 ¢ cost

Goldy (our goldfish) died on March 6. She was sick.

Mom and Dad are painting the house. It is green color.

Aunt ELLa got a new car. It is a VW. It is red. She took us for a ride in it.

GRANDMA IS GOING TO NHL NIGHT SCHOOL! She is going to learn auto fixing so she can fix her car herself. Hurray for GRANDMA !!

STAFF
Gloria Harris

A family bulletin board can be mounted on the wall near the kitchen table. This makes it very handy to be seen all the time and to be changed from time to time.

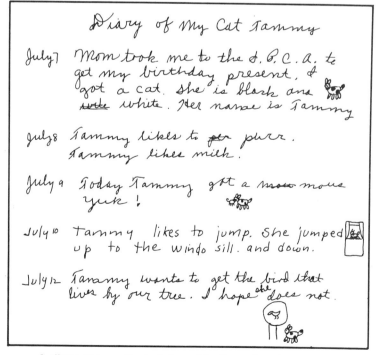

Diary of My Cat Tammy

July 7   Mom took me to the S. P. C. A. to get my birthday present, & got a cat. She is black and white. Her name is Tammy

July 8   Tammy likes to purr. Tammy likes milk.

July 9   Today Tammy got a mouse. yuk !

July 10   Tammy likes to jump. She jumped up to the windo sill. and down.

July 12   Tammy wants to get the bird that lives by our tree. I hope she does not.

A diary can motivate interest in the printed word too.

Try luring your child into the reading habit by making your own books. It isn't hard to do really, because when your books are custom-made, they are *yours* and the things *you* chose to write about. And children like this.

Titles from this library are:

THE SAD BOOK
THE HAPPY BOOK
THE THINGS I LIKE BOOK
THE THINGS I DON'T LIKE BOOK
THE ROUND BOOK

Which do you feel like reading today?

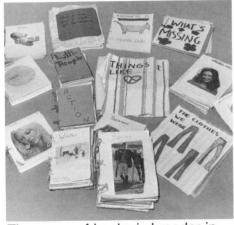

The range of books is broader in this collection:

SPRING
WINTER
THE CLOTHES WE WEAR
SMILING FACES
LITTLE PEOPLE
SHAPES
HAPPINESS IS
ACTION
WHAT I SEE WHEN I LOOK
   OUT THE WINDOW

Other possibilities to consider may include:

WORK MOM AND DAD DO
WORK OTHER PEOPLE DO
THE ALPHABET BOOK
I TRY NOT TO EAT TOO
   MUCH BOOK
THE STORY OF MY LIFE
   BOOK

READING

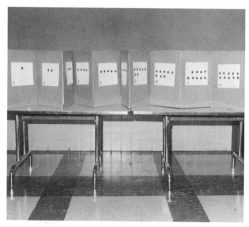

For variation in format, an accordion style is enticing to a child. You just need tape to connect the pages.

The story of my flower
By Carole Liss

MY FAMILY

MALAIKA

"My Family" book strengthens a child's self-image and feeling of "roots"—at the same time piling up indirect desires to "want to read." Other categories for bookmaking can include:

CLOTHING	WELL-KNOWN PEOPLE	ZOO ANIMALS
PETS	FOODS	FARM ANIMALS
SCHOOL SUPPLIES	THINGS OF NATURE	COMMUNITY HELPERS
HOUSES	TRANSPORTATION	PEOPLE FROM OTHER
STORES	MUSICAL INSTRUMENTS	LANDS
SPORTS	HEALTH SUPPLIES	FURNITURE

An alphabet book.

You can make books for:
- other consonants (*P,R,S,T,* etc.)
- consonant combinations (*TR* for *TREE*)
- blends (*CH* for *CHAIR*)
- short vowels (*E* for *BED*)
- long vowels (*O* for *NOSE*)

Public signs can give highly motivating lessons in "wanting to read." Perhaps your child may enjoy making a "My Sign Book" and looking for signs during walks, car rides, or in shopping plazas. Here are some:

BUS STOP
DANGER
SLOW
KEEP OFF THE GRASS
U.S. MAIL
RAILROAD CROSSING
MEN AT WORK
MERGING TRAFFIC
PLAYGROUND
SCHOOL
LADIES
MEN
BOY
GIRL
FIRE ALARM

CURB YOUR DOG
GO
SCHOOL CROSSING
CROSS HERE
EXIT
ENTRANCE
RESTAURANT
ONE WAY
ROAD REPAIR AHEAD
CAUTION
DETOUR
TELEPHONE
PUSH BUTTON FOR
   GREEN LIGHT
NO JAY WALKING

WALK—DON'T RUN
NO PARKING
ROOMS FOR RENT
VACANCY
ROAD CLOSED
GARAGE SALE
NO LOITERING
PUT TRASH HERE
AIRPORT
HOSPITAL
EMERGENCY
ROUTE 35
PET STORE
GAS STATION
SLIPPERY

READING

A homemade calendar can interest a child in "time" (days, weeks, months, a year), the seasons, birthdays, holidays and many other things. At the same time "wanting to learn to read" is indirectly encouraged.

READING

A child who has had an exhilarating experience, such as a trip to the pet store, can be led into a huge variety of things to talk about— enough to make a "whole big book, all my own."

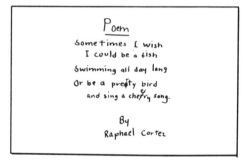

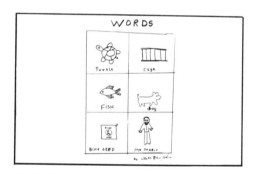

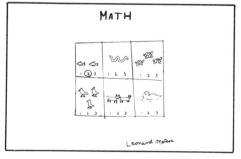

READING

Here, one "book" has been taken apart so you can see how all the pages are related and correlated with the trip—an original poem, science, new words, letter writing, math, etc.

At no time was there any coercion to do any of these pages. If any had been needed, it would have been time to stop at once!

More fun devices to "hook" a child onto the task of "wanting to read"

A story *by* a child *to* a child

or a big sister or
some high-school
student to a child

or a grandfather or grandmother to
a child

are lessons in human relations that
can never be bought.

ROPE

You can "draw" numbers and letters of the alphabet (also, fascinating pictures) with rope.

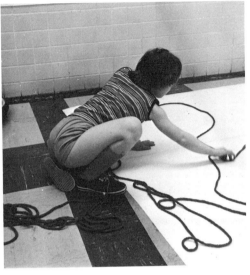

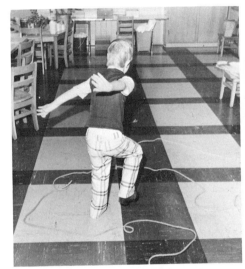

Rope is also good for "jumping over."

You can play "jump rope."

Attach some rope to blocks of wood and you can have a "chariot race."

126

SAND

Any home can have a sandbox. Do you have a carton, an old wooden box—or, why not use the dishpan?

For sand, you can bring a pailful or two from the beach or ask one of the workers at some nearby construction site. (Most workers are nice and wouldn't say no for such a small amount.)

Here are some things your child can do with sand:

- draw on it
- cook with it
- make pies
- make cakes
- make roads and highways
- dig tunnels
- make caves
- dump things
- build castles, towers, and many other things

"I love to play with sand.
It seems that when I play with sand,
Nobody ever compares me with someone else."

ROPE

SAND

Sand Substitutes

If you can't get hold of sand, here are some sand substitutes. With each you can still write your name, measure things, and construct anything you want. (When you want to erase, you just shake it up and start again !)

Sand is great, but flour is oh, so soft and fluffy !

"It feels so good to do things with my hands . . .
And I love to get them messy.
It feels so good. . . .
My hands want to go faster and faster. . . .
I hardly ever want to stop."

SAND

Sugar is a good sand substitute. (But I guess you know some problems that sugar can present !)

MORE SAND SUBSTITUTES

A box of crisp ready-to-eat rice cereal makes good "sand" (especially useful if some little character is hungry).

Rice, oatmeal, and cornmeal make excellent gravel and coal piles.

OTHER SUBSTITUTES

Lump sugar is suitable for the construction of castles, towers, lighthouses, railroads, and housing projects.

After the leaves are raked (I hope your child will help), dump a small supply into a carton to bring into the house.

SAND

SONGS AND
VERSE

Have you any wood shavings or sawdust?

SONGS AND VERSE

Songs for Learning

Is there something important you feel you would like your child to learn—his or her name, telephone number, or age? Try this fun way to do it.

Take a familiar tune, change the words to whatever it is you want your child to learn, and sing it over and over again. (Even if you think you can't sing, sing anyway.)

Sing when doing the dishes. Sing when you take a shower. And then, listen—your child may soon be singing along with you.

Objective: to learn telephone number

Familiar tune:
Twinkle, Twinkle, Little Star

Twin-kle, twin-kle, lit-tle star
8   7   6   4   87   2

How I won-der what you are
8 7 6   4   8   7   2

Up a-bove the world so high
8 7 6   4   8   7   2

Like a dia-mond in the sky
8 7 6   4   8 7   2

Twin-kle, twin-kle, lit-tle star
8   7   6   4 87   2

How I won-der what you are
8 7 6   4   8   7   2

Objective: to learn name

Familiar tune:
Mary Had a Little Lamb

Mary Burchfield is my name
              is my name
              is my name
Mary Burchfield is my name
Mary is my name.

Objective: to learn one's sex

Familiar tune:
The Farmer in the Dell

Michael is a boy
Michael is a boy
Michael is a boy
Michael is a boy

Linda is a girl, etc.

Objective: to learn about daily routine

Familiar tune:
The Farmer in the Dell

In the morning I wake up
In the morning I wake up
In the morning I wake up
In the morning I wake up

Then I brush my teeth, etc.

Objective: to rote count to ten

Familiar tune: Jingle Bells

1-2-3
4-5-6
7-8-9-10
1-2-3
4-5-6
7-8-9-10

Objective: to learn to identify coins

Familiar tune: Go Tell Aunt Rhody

I've got a penny
I've got a penny
I've got a penny
Penny, penny, penny.

I've got a nickel, etc.

Objective: to learn parts of the body

Familiar tune:
Row, Row, Row Your Boat

Touch, touch, touch your nose
Touch your nose like this
Touch, touch, touch your nose
Touch your nose like this

Touch, touch, touch your knees, etc.

Objective: to learn right and left hands and feet

Familiar tune: Frère Jacques

Raise your right hand
Raise your right hand
Raise your right hand
Raise your right hand
Raise your right hand
Raise your right hand
Raise your right hand
Raise your right hand

Raise your right foot, etc.

Objective: to learn days of week

Familiar tune: Yankee Doodle

Monday Tuesday Wednesday
Thursday
Friday Saturday Sunday
Monday Tuesday Wednesday
Thursday
Friday Saturday Sunday

Objective: to become familiar with musical instruments

Familiar tune:
Did You Ever See a Lassie?

I can play a trumpet
a trumpet
a trumpet
I can play a trumpet
Toot toot toot toot

I can play a violin
a violin
a violin
I can play a violin
Hm hm hm hm

Etc.

Objective: to learn names of parents, sisters, etc.

Familiar tune: Are You Sleeping?

John is my father
John is my father
John is my father
John is my father
John is my father
John is my father
John is my father
John is my father

Gloria is my mother, etc.

Objective: to become familiar with animal sounds

Familiar tune:
London Bridge Is Falling Down

Tell me how the kitty talks
kitty talks
kitty talks
Tell me how the kitty talks
Me ow   Me ow   Me ow   Me ow

Tell me how the doggy talks, etc.

Objective: to learn common terms of courtesy

Familiar tune:
Happy Birthday to You

Good morning to you
Good morning to you
Good morning to you
Good morning to you

Good night to you
Good night to you
Good night to you
Good night to you

Etc.

Objective: to learn one's age

Familiar tune:
Happy Birthday to You

How old am I?
How old am I?
How old am I?
How old am I?

I'm ____ years old
I'm ____ years old
I'm ____ years old
I'm ____ years old

Objective:
to learn the alphabet by rote

Familiar tune: The ABC Song

A   B   C   D   E   F   G
H   I   J   K   L   M   N   O   P
Q   R   S   and   T   U   V
W   X   and   Y   and   Z
Now I know my ABCs.
Tell me what you think of me.

Objective: to learn meaning of action words

Familiar tune:
Go Round and Round the Village
Let's walk around the table
Let's walk around the table
Let's walk around the table
Let's walk and walk and walk.

Let's jump around the table, etc.

SONGS AND VERSE

133

Nursery Rhymes

Just about everyone—a miner in Kentucky, the bus driver, any astronaut, and (yes !) the president of the United States, too, knows five, six, and maybe even most of these foolish jingly nursery rhymes. They are built (somehow) into our culture, and it may be hard to trace back how any of us got to learn them.

Never mind that the words don't seem to make much sense. See how the children respond *immediately* to their bouncy rhythms:

hopping,
skipping,
jumping,
galloping,
walking,
swinging gently.

Your child may be too young to read them, but you can expect such strong requests as, *"Say it again ! Say it again !"*

Roses are red,
Violets are blue,
Sugar is sweet,
And so are you.

I asked my mother for fifty cents
To see the elephant jump the fence.
He jumped so high, he touched the sky
And didn't get back till the Fourth of July.

I made you look,
I made you look,
I made you buy a penny book.

Sticks and stones may break my bones,
But names will never hurt me.
When I die, then you'll cry
For the names you called me.

A knife and a fork
A bottle and a cork
And that's the way to spell
New York.

I had a dog, his name was Rover.
When he rolled, he rolled in the clover.
When he died, he died all over.
Goodbye, Rover.

I had a little calf
And that's half.
I put him in the stall
And tied him to the wall
And that's all.

I know something I won't tell.
Three little monkeys in a peanut shell.
One can sing and one can dance
And one can make a pair of pants.

Good night.
Sleep tight.
Don't let the mosquitoes bite.

There was an old man named Michael Finnegan.
He grew a long beard right on his chinnegan.
Along came a wind and blew it in again—
Poor old Michael Finnegan. Begin again.

One for the money,
Two for the show,
Three to get ready,
And four to go.

Monkey on the railroad.
Monkey on the fence.
Monkey get your hair cut,
Fifteen cents.

Monkey in the barnyard.
Monkey in the stable.
Monkey get your hair cut
Soon as you are able.

1, 2, 3, 4, 5,
I caught a fish alive;
6, 7, 8, 9, 10 !
I let it go again.

If you ever, ever, ever, ever meet a whale,
You must never, never, never, never grab him by the tail.
If you ever, ever, ever, ever grab him by his tail,
You will never, never, never, never meet another whale.

Deedle, deedle, dumpling, my son John,
He went to sleep with his stockings on;
One shoe off and one shoe on.
Deedle, deedle, dumpling, my son John.

Hippity hop to the barbershop,
To get a stick of candy.
One for you and one for me,
And one for Sister Mandy.

Solomon Grundy
Born on Monday
Christened on Tuesday
Married on Wednesday
Took ill on Thursday
Worse on Friday
Died on Saturday
Buried on Sunday
This is the end of Solomon Grundy.

Wouldn't it be funny,
Wouldn't it be now,
If the dog said "moo"
And the cow said "bowwow"
And the cat sang and whistled
And the bird said "meow"?
Wouldn't it be funny?
Wouldn't it now?

Pretty little red bird
Dressed so fine,
Got a little red coat
Just like mine.

Spell Tennessee:
One-a-see
Two-a-see
Three-a-see
Four-a-see
Five-a-see
Six-a-see
Seven-a-see
Eight-a-see
Nine-a-see
Tenn-e-ssee

It's hippity hop to bed.
I'd rather sit up instead.
But when father says "must"
There's nothing but just
Go hippity hop to bed.

Cry, baby, cry,
Take your little shirttail
And wipe your little eye
And go tell your mommy
To give you a piece of pie.

A.B.C.
Double down D.
The cat's in the cupboard
And can't see me.

Thirty days hath September,
April, June, and November;
Save February, the rest have thirty-one
Unless you hear from Washington.

Ladybug, ladybug, fly away home,
Your house is on fire, your children will burn;
All but the youngest, whose name is Ann,
And she hid herself 'neath the frying pan.

A flea and a fly in a flue
Were imprisoned, so what could they do?
Said the fly, "Let us flee !"
"Let us fly !" said the flea.
So they flew through a flaw in the flue.

A boy stood on the burning deck,
Eating peanuts by the peck;
His father called him, he wouldn't go,
Because he loved his peanuts so.

No more pencils, no more books,
No more teacher's nasty looks.

There once was a guy by the name of Jack,
Pitched his tent on a railroad track;
The 7:15 came round the bend.
What kind of flowers are you going to send?

Listen my children and you shall hear
Of the midnight ride of Paul Revere.
He got in his car and stepped on the gas,
The bottom fell out and he fell on the grass.

I went downtown
To see Mrs. Brown.
She gave me a nickel
To buy a pickle.
The pickle was sour,
So I bought a flower.
The flower was dead,
So I bought some thread.
The thread was thin,
So I bought a pin.
The pin was sharp,
So I bought a harp.
The harp wouldn't play,
So I gave it away
And went back downtown
To see Mrs. Brown.

One, two, buckle my shoe;
Three, four, shut the door;
Five, six, pick up sticks;
Seven, eight, lay them straight;
Nine, ten, a big fat hen.

Ask me no questions,
And I'll tell you no lies;
But bring me those apples
And I'll make you some pies.

Johnny's it,
And had a fit,
And didn't know how
To get over it.

Hay is for horses,
Straw is for cows,
Milk is for babies
For crying out loud.

Two's a couple,
Three's a crowd,
Four on the sidewalk
Is never allowed.

Early to bed,
Early to rise,
Makes a man (or woman)
Healthy, wealthy, and wise.

Choral Readings

If you like, you can break up some of the rhymes into "choral readings." For example, you can take one part and your child another; sometimes you can go together.

I have selected the following because they happen to have been favorites of my own children and also some of my students.

• Enjoy the magical pictures they bring.

• Listen to the musical sounds they bring to our ears.

• But mostly, enjoy the "doing it together," where the real value lies.

BOTH:	Little Robin Redbreast
	sat upon a tree.
PARENT:	Up went pussy cat.
CHILD:	Down went he.
PARENT:	Down went pussy cat.
CHILD:	Away Robin ran.
BOTH:	Said Little Robin Redbreast,
	"Catch me if you can !"

PARENT:	Whisky, frisky,
CHILD:	Hippity hop.
PARENT:	Up he goes
CHILD:	To the treetop !
PARENT:	Whirly, twirly,
CHILD:	Round and round,
BOTH:	Down he scampers
	To the ground.

PARENT:	What does the hail say?
CHILD:	"Knock ! Knock !"
PARENT:	What does the rain say?
CHILD:	"Pit ! Pit !"
PARENT:	What does the sleet say?
CHILD:	"Sh ! Sh !"
PARENT:	What does the wind say?
CHILD:	"Whoo ! Whoo !"

PARENT:	Spring is:
CHILD:	Showery, flowery, bowery.
PARENT:	Summer is:
CHILD:	Hoppy, croppy, floppy.
PARENT:	Autumn is:
CHILD:	Wheezy, sneezy, freezy.
PARENT:	Winter is:
CHILD:	Slippery, drippy, nippy.

PARENT:	All around the cobbler's bench
CHILD:	The monkey chased the weasel.
PARENT:	The monkey thought 'twas all in fun
BOTH:	Pop ! Goes the weasel.
PARENT:	Johnny has the whooping cough,
CHILD:	Mary has the measles.
PARENT:	That's the way the money goes.
BOTH:	Pop ! Goes the weasel.

PARENT: I have a little pussy, CHILD: Her coat is silver gray. PARENT: She lives in a great wide meadow, CHILD: And she never runs away. PARENT: She always is a pussy, CHILD: She'll never be a cat. PARENT: Because she's a pussy willow. BOTH: Now what do you think of that?	PARENT: Pussy cat, pussy cat, where have you been? CHILD: I've been to London to visit the queen. PARENT: Pussy cat, pussy cat, what did you there? CHILD: I frightened the little mouse under the chair.

PARENT: There was a crooked man CHILD: And he walked a crooked mile. PARENT: He found a crooked sixpence CHILD: On a crooked stile. PARENT: He bought a crooked cat, CHILD: Which caught a crooked mouse. BOTH: And they all lived together in a little crooked house.	PARENT: Once I saw a little bird CHILD: Come hop, hop, hop. PARENT: So I cried, "Little bird, CHILD: Will you stop, stop, stop?" PARENT: I was going to the window CHILD: To say, "How do you do?" BOTH: But he shook his little tail, And far away he flew.

PARENT: Said the first little chicken,
With a queer little squirm,
CHILD: "I wish I could find a fat little worm !"
PARENT: Said the next little chicken,
With an odd little shrug,
CHILD: "I wish I could find a fat little slug !"
PARENT: Said the third little chicken,
With a sharp little squeal,
CHILD: "I wish I could find some nice yellow
meal !"
PARENT: Said the fourth little chicken,
With a small sigh of grief,
CHILD: "I wish I could find a little green leaf !"
PARENT: Said a fifth little chicken
With a faint little moan,
CHILD: "I wish I could find a wee gravel
stone !"
BOTH: "Now see here," said the mother
From the green garden patch,
"If you want any breakfast
Just come here and scratch !"

SONGS AND VERSE

SPOOLS

PARENT: Let us try to be polite
CHILD: In everything we do.
PARENT: Remember always to say "please"
CHILD: And don't forget "thank you."

SPOOLS

A collection of spools will take a shorter time to collect if you alert friends, relatives, seamstresses, and tailor shops to save them for you. (You will be surprised at the variety of sizes they come in and the number of exciting things you can do with them !)

If you look carefully on the left side of this picture, you will see the beginnings of a necklace. It happens to be part of a valuable set of jewelry (which will include a bracelet and a belt) for "Mom's birthday."

Spools are excellent for towers to "see how high you can get them before they crash down." They are also good for colorful totem poles (with or without faces).

Spools squiggle and don't always go where you want them to. But it's fun to roll them anyway to see where they *do* land.

These spools are from a knitting mill. This is the City Hall.

These are 33mm film spools and are "workers in a factory." (If you have a typewriter, you might want to save the spools from the ribbons, too.)

STONES

Wherever you go

- in the city
- in the country
- to the beach
- up a mountain

you'll find all kinds of stones.

- flat ones
- round ones
- long skinny ones
- stones with pretty colors and designs

You might even find a stone that has an old, old plant or animal buried in it !

Can you find a stone that is good for writing with on sidewalks?

- Save your stones for things to do on a rainy day. You can store them outside your house and nothing will happen to them.

You can paint on a stone.

You can "write" your name with beans on a stone.

You can make a doll with stones.

You can glue your favorite shells on stones.

TIRES

Tire tubes are for contemplation.

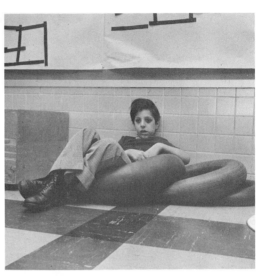

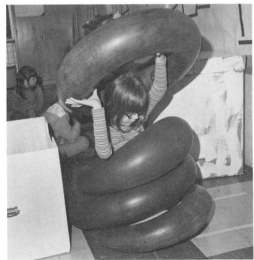

Tire tubes are for hiding in.
If you tie several together and lay them
horizontally, you can hide in a tunnel.

And tire tubes are for jumping in and
out of.

TRIPS

Often we forget that something commonplace to us can be completely new to a child. There surely must be loads of exciting things in your neighborhood or local community to delight a child's eyes and ears—and things to smell, taste, and touch.

If you look over the newspaper or call your museum, there might be notices of special events taking place or some free guided tours open to the public. Sometimes events are posted in public buildings, Y's, or libraries.

Why not decide on one place to visit, take the car or drive out by bus—AND MAKE A DAY OF IT !

- Be sure your child sits by the window so he or she can see things passing by.

- Also, bring a good lunch—or, if you can afford it, eat in a nearby restaurant for a treat.

This is David with the prize rabbit (isn't it adorable?) at the Erie County Fair. Its owner allowed David to cuddle the rabbit—and I don't think he will ever forget this !

It's really of no special significance that these goats are being fed (they are probably overstuffed already anyway). What is of importance is that there is a very good feeling when one helps and cares for a living creature.

THINGS TO SEE AND/OR DO ON A TRIP

- dirt road
- lighthouse
- fish hatchery
- dairy-cattle auction
- flower market
- sidewalk art show
- lilacs in bloom
- strawberry patch
- pigs
- cave
- cherry orchard
- stockyards
- haystack
- freshly picked peaches
- drawbridge
- wild berries
- Indian corn festival
- skunk cabbage
- blue sky
- candy factory
- dog show
- stained-glass church windows
- flower nursery

- outdoor mural
- protest march
- religious church service
- Indian reservation
- chicks peeping
- red sunset
- go for a subway ride
- wintergreen
- bridge
- fossils
- reservoir
- dam
- ride a tractor
- go on a nature-trail hike
- climb a hill
- farmers' market
- cheese factory
- quarry
- lumberyard
- dog kennel
- fort
- fish cannery
- pier
- irrigation ditch

- viaduct
- rooster crowing
- go for a boat ride along harbor
- Puerto Rican Festival
- hooting owl
- chipmunks
- dog pound
- weeds on the shore
- St. Patrick's Day parade
- rippling water
- horses neighing
- listen to the sound of the ocean
- peepers and frogs
- soybeans
- ducks
- calves
- pebbles
- shells
- field of clover
- streams
- logging
- trees in the cemetery
- restored village
- Little Red Schoolhouse
- vineyards
- wheat
- snakes
- maple-sugar farm
- turkey farm
- mine
- burnt-out area
- waterfalls
- beaver dam
- Chinese neighborhood
- Labor Day parade
- tugboat
- airport
- trillium
- sculpture court
- mural
- violets

Then, of course, there are always the
LET'S-SEE-WHAT'S-GOING-ON-AROUND-THE-BLOCK TRIPS.

- freshly cut grass
- hot tar
- wet dog
- rays of sunshine through the clouds
- frosty windows
- sound of thunder
- men laying sewers
- men repairing telephone wires
- men laying electric cables
- bulldozer
- men collecting garbage
- thick fog starting to roll in
- creaking of a porch swing
- streak of a jet through the sky
- someone practicing the piano
- the hum of insects
- curtains in a window
- high grass
- spider
- cars in a driveway
- stars
- pigeons cooing
- screeching screen door
- church bells ringing
- steak broiling
- wind whistling
- mailboxes
- the sky
- fresh yellow paint
- porch railings
- slamming of garbage cans
- clover
- shadows
- squirrels
- cocoons
- old boards
- Queen Anne's lace
- fire hydrants
- gentle breeze
- tree trunks
- dandelions
- caterpillar
- traffic signs
- political posters

- children singing
- hopscotch
- raking of leaves
- watering of lawns
- washing of porch steps
- taking of cookies over to a neighbor
- shucking of corn for dinner
- sweet-pea trellis
- big crane
- power shovel
- bricks being laid
- cement being poured
- telephone lines
- kites flying
- new roof
- fences
- delivery trucks
- babies in playpens
- new grass coming up
- the mailman
- ladders
- washing windows
- ball game
- children roller skating
- bicycles
- jogging
- gum wrappers
- vacant lots
- a feather
- TVs playing from an open window
- clocks chiming
- footsteps
- policeman's whistle
- dogs barking
- street lights
- ants
- butterflies
- stars
- windows in the attic
- worms
- seed pods
- animal tracks
- babies in buggies
- mother calling children to bed

WATER

Don't feel bad if you can't take your child to the beach—it isn't always possible. Besides, your child can have a lot of fun (and also learn many things) right at home with a dishpan of water. And outdoors there is always the hose water to run in and out of.

If you are lucky enough to have a backyard, why not give up a small part of it, dig a hole, (with your child's help, of course) and let your child have a magnificent *mudhole* for pies and other delicacies.

I am a little saddened that mud-pie baking is slowly becoming a lost art. IT DEFINITELY SHOULD BE REVIVED !

Isn't it remarkable that children don't seem to care *what they paint on* or *with what?* For example, here is Christine "painting" on an old newspaper with water !

Other possibilities to "paint" include: the refrigerator, the bathroom floor, and the basement floor and walls.

If you need a river for boats, you can saw an old tire through the middle.

For outdoor jobs, the driveway, sidewalk, porch steps, and fence are always in need of doing. (One intriguing aspect of water painting is that the "paint" marks always disappear when they dry.)

WOOD

The scrap boxes in lumberyards can be treasure chests for free building blocks. One nearby lumber company incinerates scraps every week—mahogany ! cherry ! walnut !—just because no one asks for them.

Is there a house being built in the neighborhood? Perhaps you can ask one of the workers for leftover pieces.

Only a little sanding to get rid of splinters, and your child is ready for

- pyramids
- trains
- bridges
- skyscrapers
- apartment houses
- airports
- factories

and hundreds of other projects triggered off by a fertile mind.

These particular blocks were made for our own children over thirty years ago and are still good for my students today.

Alex may hit his fingers a few times as he tries to hammer a nail into the wood, but he'll learn many things in the process. (When he learns to hammer well, he may wish to nail two pieces of wood together to make a book end.)

Don't you think these sawed-off pieces from an old wooden broomstick make a tempting birthday cake?

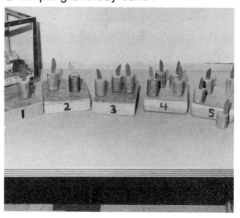

Soft wire, the wire twists that close off plastic bags, or pipe cleaners—mounted on wood—can be squeezed, bent, bumped, twisted, and curled.

If you want to display those precious shells, pine cones, or stones found on the hike, wood makes a beautiful natural background.

Line blocks (small blocks of wood from which string is suspended, helping workmen to align bricks) are usually available at building supply stores. They are given out free of charge to workers and often to children who are —of course—workers too.

Line blocks make excellent sky scrapers and apartment houses.

There are so many things to do—so many things to have.
Yet, with all these things—when all is said and done

    In that very instant

        when you look right at the child
        when the child looks right at you
        when your eyes meet
        and the child feels

    "YOU KNOW I'M HERE. I COUNT !"

This is the most important thing you can give your child.

ANIMALS

BAGS

BIRDS

BOTTLES

BOXES

BRICKS

BUTTONS

CANS

CARDBOARD

CLAY

CLOTHING

DANCE

FINGER PLAYS

FOOD

FURNITURE

INSECTS

KITCHENWARE

MUSICAL INSTRUMENTS

PANTOMIME

PAPER

PLANTS

PLASTIC

PUPPETS

READING

ROPE

SAND

SONGS AND VERSE

SPOOLS

STONES

TIRES

TRIPS

WATER

WOOD

1. Place your thumb on the
   tab for the section you
   want.

2. Riffle through the pages
   until you come to the
   corresponding tab.